RESPECT FOR LIFE

in Medicine, Philosophy, and the Law

THE ALVIN AND FANNY BLAUSTEIN
THALHEIMER LECTURES
1975

Stephen F. Barker, Editor

RESPECT FOR LIFE

in Medicine, Philosophy, and the Law

OWSEI TEMKIN

WILLIAM K. FRANKENA

SANFORD H. KADISH

The Johns Hopkins University Press

Baltimore and London

Chapter 3 was originally published in *California Law Review* 64 (1976): 871–901,
copyright © 1976, Sanford H. Kadish.

Manufactured in the United States of America

The Johns Hopkins University Press, Baltimore, Maryland 21218
The Johns Hopkins Press Ltd., London

Library of Congress Catalog Card Number 76-47366
ISBN 0-8018-1942-3

Library of Congress Cataloging in Publication data
will be found on the last printed page of this book.

CONTENTS

PREFACE

The idea of respect for life has long been a central notion in the scheme of values of Western civilization. Despite many lapses in practice—crimes committed showing comtempt for life, sometimes on a terrifying scale—the idea of respect for life has continued to be regarded as affording a distinctive ideal standard, which many still believe sets much of Western civilization apart from other civilizations, whose ideals are perhaps less humane. This idea has informed Western attitudes concerning what is morally permissible and what ought to be legally permitted; especially so with regard to the conduct of medical practice.

Recently, there has been a marked increase of interest in questions of medical ethics, both on the part of the general public and on the part of scholars in philosophy, medicine, and law. One cause of this increased interest has been the more permissive attitudes and new legal decisions which have made acceptable certain medical procedures—especially abortion—which previously had been considered to be ethically impermissible. Liberal-minded people who seek to justify these procedures find themselves puzzlingly confronted by the principle of respect for life, to which they also wish to give allegiance, yet which seems to stand opposed to these procedures. Another cause of this increased interest in medical ethics comes from technological advances in medical care that give rise to ethical problems not previously encountered. For example, patients whose capacity for higher mental functions has been permanently lost can now sometimes be kept alive indefinitely: to what extent ought this to be done? Would euthanasia conflict with the principle of respect for life, or would letting such patients die do so?

In recent discussions of such issues in medical ethics, we find the liberal, more-or-less utilitarian outlook—which has been becoming more and more widespread—moving into at least partial conflict with the traditional humane ideal of respect for life. This latter ideal, quasi-religious in character, seems to demand that we take a stand on principle and declare that certain ethical and legal issues may not be settled by means of cost-benefit analysis. This demand has a powerful and authoritative appeal to many of us, which even the momentum of utilitarian ways of thinking cannot wholly overcome.

Yet this idea, or principle, of respect for life is itself obscure and controversial. What did it mean in earlier times, and what should it mean for us today?

The three contributors to this volume approach the idea of respect for life from different perspectives, seeking in different ways to shed light upon its meaning. Dr. Temkin's approach is through the history of medicine, discussing ways in which early Western medicine understood the duty to respect life. Professor Frankena's approach is in terms of philosophy, drawing essential distinctions among ways in which respect for life has been understood, and recommending his own interpretation of how moral philosophy should define it. Dean Kadish approaches the topic through consideration of our criminal law, seeking to map an underlying coherency in the way the law treats diverse cases of the taking of life—thereby exhibiting what respect for life means in law. Taken together, the three contributions aim to help us toward a clearer and richer appreciation of what the idea of respect for life has meant and does mean for us.

The three lectures which this volume comprises were delivered at the Johns Hopkins University in the spring of 1975, as the fourth series of the Alvin and Fanny Blaustein Thalheimer Lectures. These lectures have been made possible by a gift from the Thalheimer Foundation.

Both Alvin Thalheimer (1894–1965) and Fanny Blaustein Thalheimer (1895–1957) were prominent citizens of Baltimore. Alvin Thalheimer earned a Ph.D. in philosophy at Johns Hopkins, and published two books in philosophy; he taught for a time at Johns Hopkins but then made his principal career in business. He actively served in numerous charitable, educational, and public organizations, especially the Associated Jewish Charities, the Baltimore Council of Social Agencies, and the Maryland State Welfare Board. His wife, Fanny Blaustein Thalheimer, studied painting at the Maryland Institute and long served on the Maryland State Board of Education. She also was active in many civic and philanthropic organizations in Baltimore.

Stephen F. Barker

RESPECT FOR LIFE

in Medicine, Philosophy, and the Law

ONE

Owsei Temkin

THE IDEA OF RESPECT FOR LIFE
IN THE HISTORY OF MEDICINE

1.

In 1948, when the horrors of the Nazi concentration camps were fresh in everybody's mind, the World Medical Association adopted what is known as the Declaration of Geneva. On admission to his profession the young doctor was to pledge himself "to consecrate [his] life to the service of humanity." Among other pledges, he promised: "I will maintain the utmost respect for human life, from the time of conception; even under threat, I will not use my medical knowledge contrary to the laws of humanity."[1] The inhumanity of the preceding years shed light on the meaning of the laws of humanity. Now there would not be much doubt how the doctor's utmost respect for human life would direct his behavior; he would do absolutely nothing that could harm life or extinguish it. In particular, it is to be assumed that he would not practice abortion, he would not provide euthanasia, and he would not perform experiments detrimental to human beings.

The social and moral turmoil of the years since World War II has raised new debates, in the heat of which "respect for life" has

1. Notes may be found on pp. 19-23.

1

tended to become a slogan. As is the way with slogans, it hides the complexity of underlying thought in order to concentrate moral force on action. Our discourse, however, will devote itself first of all to this complexity. It will not ask whether, when, and how life *should* be respected in medicine. In an analytical mood, we shall try to illuminate the content of the idea, and we shall do so by looking at some of its manifestations in the history of Western medicine, as a profession dedicated to the practice and discipline of healing.

Those, then, who expect a message will be disappointed, and so will historians who expect a narrative of the development of the idea through the ages. Moral ideas do not necessarily unfold with the flow of time. They have a tendency to cling to what is old, just because it is old and thereby hallowed, to what presents itself as a tradition to be invoked or refuted. We shall, therefore, start with the formation of what we shall call "the medical tradition." Since this took place in Greece and Rome between 400 B.C. and A.D. 200, we shall, like the academic speaker of old, have to begin with: "The ancient Greeks already . . ." The audience used to respond by resigning itself to forbearance, and everybody tried to make himself as comfortable as the hard chairs would allow.

We shall indeed have to come back to the ancients again and again. But considering that, fundamentally, the Geneva Declaration is an adaptation of the Hippocratic Oath, and that the oath is repeated by the graduating students of many medical schools, often in the translation of the Greek text ascribed to "the father of medicine"—considering this, we shall see that in medical ethics the ancients not only preceded us but are very much with us.

2.

In taking the Hippocratic Oath, the young physician not only promises to act for the good of his patients and to keep them from harm and injustice, but he also states: "I will neither give a deadly drug to anybody if asked for it, nor will I make a suggestion to this effect. Similarly, I will not give to a woman an abortive remedy. In purity and holiness I will guard my life and my art."[2] No mention is made of the economic, social, or national status of the patients, and the physician, who is an expert in the power of drugs, forswears participation in murder, suicide, and abortion. It is generally accepted that the oath was not written by Hippocrates, who lived around 400 B.C. It did not express the common medical ethics of that time. According to Ludwig Edelstein, it reflects the thoughts of the Pythagoreans of the fourth century B.C. By the first century after Christ it had become a well-known document, referred to by the Roman Scribonius Largus and by Soranus, a Greek practicing in Rome at the end of the century.

Soranus relates a medical controversy over the use of contraceptives and the practice of abortion: "One party banishes abortives, citing the testimony of Hippocrates, who says: 'I will give to no one an abortive,' . . . because it is the specific task of medicine to guard and preserve what has been engendered by nature."[3] In referring to medicine as the guardian of life, the statement defines respect for life as a general medical responsibility. "The other party," Soranus continues, "prescribes abortives, but with discrimination, that is, they do not prescribe them when a person wishes to destroy the embryo because of adultery or out of consideration for youthful beauty; but only to prevent subsequent danger in parturition." With this latter party, which held similar views about the use of contraceptives, Soranus agreed. In modern terms, one party rejected all abortion, whereas the other party allowed therapeutic abortion. Economic reasons were not mentioned, probably because they did not exist for the rich clientele of the highly accomplished physicians whose writings have come down to us.

Scribonius Largus took the Hippocratic prohibition of abortion to be an education toward humanity. He who deemed it wrong to injure a fetus, which, after all, held only the promise of future human life, would certainly deem it even more criminal to harm a completed human being.[4]

The fame of the oath was rivaled only by that of the *Aphorisms*, another work ascribed to Hippocrates. This work begins with the well-known words: "Life is short, the art is long [*ars longa, vita brevis* in the Latin translation], opportunity fleeting, experience perilous, and the crisis difficult."[5] Here was rich food for the commentators! What did Hippocrates mean by calling experience perilous? As Galen, the great physician-philosopher of the second century, explained, the danger lay in dealing with the human body. "For in the medical art, unlike the other arts, the material is not brick, clay, wood, stone, earthenware, or hides." Those dealing with this kind of material could work without causing harm, even if they handled it badly. "But in the human body, to try out what has not been tested is not without peril, in case a bad experiment lead to the destruction of the whole organism."[6]

Let us now add an example referring to euthanasia, which is all the more instructive because it is taken from a novel, *The Golden Ass*, by Apuleius, a contemporary of Galen's.[7] It brings into relief the physician's respect for life as being above and beyond the demands of the law. A physician, we are told, was asked for a fast-acting poison, allegedly "for a sick man in the throes of an inveterate, intractable disease who longed to escape the torture of his life,"[8] in reality for the purpose of murdering him. The physician sold a potion, but when later an innocent man was accused of murder, the physician revealed that the potion had only been a sleeping draught and not a deadly poison, "because he did not believe it proper for his calling to be instrumental in bringing death to anybody, and because he had been taught that medicine had been invented not for the destruction of man but for his welfare."[9]

If poison had really been demanded for suicide, which the Roman law did not forbid,[10] the physician would not have committed a punishable act by providing it. But apart from distrusting the buyer, the physician did not believe that his profession allowed poisoning, even for the sake of suicidal euthanasia. And, indeed, the seemingly dead man was awakened, the criminals suitably punished, and the conscientious physician rewarded.

Sufficient material has now been gathered to prove the existence of a tradition which, in its uncompromising form, did not sanction any limit to the respect for life, not even therapeutic abortion, an exception allowed by the more liberal wing. This tradition is very much with us; even the arguments used are still alive. Many physicians feel the tradition to be binding upon themselves, and many laymen expect it to be binding for the physician. Perhaps the impression has even been conveyed that we have said all there is to be said about respect for life, at least in principle, so that only details are to be added. This impression would be misleading. The tradition is ambiguous. It has had to confront other demands that influenced it, and it has not been free from contradictions within itself.

3.

However dedicated to his profession a physician may be, he has to live in a world that makes multiple claims on him. Besides the private obligations to his family, the state is likely to make demands, if not of actual service, at least of loyalty. For this, both the forementioned Scribonius Largus and Hippocrates—not the historical Hippocrates, who lived at the time of sovereign Greek city-states in which the peripatetic physicians were strangers, but the Hippocrates of the legend that began to grow around him in Hellenistic times of strengthened common Greek patriotism —give classical examples. The legend has the king of Persia, the traditional enemy of the Greeks, look for a physician who will stop the plague decimating the Persian army. The king's agent approaches Hippocrates with the promise of great wealth and high rank. Whereupon Hippocrates replies, "We enjoy food, garments, housing, and everything essential to life. It is not right for me to share the Persians' wealth, or to liberate from disease barbarians who are the enemies of the Greeks. Fare thee well."[11]

By the early first century, Scribonius Largus has elaborated the relationship between medicine and patriotic duty. Their profession demands that physicians have compassion and humanity, lest they be detested by gods and men. Because medicine does not measure men by their wealth or rank, but promises that it will give ready help to all who implore it and will never harm anybody, a physician properly bound to medicine by an oath will not give bad medicaments, even to enemies. "But," our author says, "when circumstances [the state?] so demand, the physician as a soldier and a good citizen will pursue them [i.e., the enemies] by any means."[12]

In the Second World War, medical research into diseases that were of great military importance was kept secret, lest the enemy profit from it. Few researchers probably realized that they were following in the footsteps of the legendary Hippocrates, who counted his refusal to help the Persian army the equivalent of a battle won at sea.[13] Scribonius Largus apparently experienced no difficulty in reconciling his twofold obligations as physician and citizen; in his capacity of physician he would not harm the enemy (prisoners of war?), but in his capacity of good citizen and soldier he would fight him.[14] The potential difficulty of reconciling two different claims on the same person has been illustrated by those physicians who, during the Vietnam War, gave their Hippocratic Oath as a reason against serving in the army. Presumably they felt that, being physicians, they should be nothing but physicians, and that nothing should be allowed to put limits on the respect they owed to life.

Different claims need not always be in opposition, and good citizenship could, and did, broaden the scope of respect for life. Thus the medieval doctor advised his fellow citizens—not just his patients—how to protect themselves from the plague.[15] In the early twentieth century, participation in public health, traditionally in the hands of lay administrators, could still be thought of as an obligation of the physician as a good citizen rather than as his duty as a medical man.[16]

The claims of religion, at least, we would expect always to support the medical respect for life. But even here there is no pre-established harmony. Physicians knew that a despondent patient was not in a good condition to win the battle for life and that the physician should lift up his sagging spirits. In the words of an early medieval author, "Even as light illuminates a home and makes men see in dark shadows, so a cheerful physician turns sorrow and sadness into joy, and comforts all of the members of his patient and restores his spirits."[17] But the Church, which valued the welfare of the soul more highly than the life of the body, demanded that the physician tell the patient the truth and see to it that he put his house in order and confess to the priest.[18] In obeying this demand, the physician endangered his patient's life; in disobeying, he endangered the patient's soul, as well as his own. The medieval doctor found a way out of the dilemma. He would arrange for confession before entering the sickroom. "For if this is discussed after the medical examination, the patient will begin to despair of his health, because he will believe that you also despair."[19] The French physician of the Enlightenment was advised to give an unsuspecting, mortally ill patient an inkling of his true condition, just enough "to make him aware of his duties and make him fulfill them." What those duties were was left open.[20]

The Protestant physician did not need to consider any priest, and so Thomas Percival, in his famous Code of Medical Ethics, which appeared in Manchester in 1803, declared: "The physician should be the messenger of hope and comfort to the sick; that by such cordials to the drooping spirit, he may smooth the bed of death, revive expiring life, and counteract the depressing influence of those maladies which rob the physician of fortitude, and the Christian of consolation."[21] Percival's English Code formed the basis of the code of ethics of 1847 of the American Medical Association. The whole passage was reprinted except for the end, which now read: "those maladies which often disturb the tranquillity of the most resigned in their last moments."[22] This could be acceptable to Catholics, Protestants, Jews, and freethinkers alike, and was proper for a society in which state and religion were separated.

Through all these examples the medical tradition takes death to be the ultimate enemy. Dying is opposed to the very last. The doctor encourages the patient's will to live, for to prepare him for death is not his medical duty. He must, of course, be tactful. The ancient physician who had cited to his despairing patient the Homeric line (*Iliad* 21.107): "Patroclus also died, and he was much better than you," was held up as a horrid example of how not to act.[23] There remained the vexing problem of whether the patient ought to be told the truth, or whether this should be left to his relatives. But apart from tact and the silent respect paid to the dying, the *ars moriendi*, the art of dying, was in the hands of ministers and philosophers rather than physicians.

Terminal illness has become a special medical problem for us today. We are more aware of dying as a process inherent in the process of life; we speak of a death instinct in man, and the beginning and ending of life have become medical and legal issues.

4.

The state and the Church, or, social and religious life, have appeared before us as historical forces that molded the contours of respect for life in medicine. To speak of contours is to use a spatial metaphor—the medical tradition is inside and the other forces impinge on it from outside—that is somewhat simplistic, but it is analytically useful and allows us to turn now to the contradictions *within* the medical tradition.

As an example we cite the case of the infant that cannot pass through the birth canal, be it that the mother's pelvis is too narrow, be it that hydrocephalus has pathologically enlarged the infant's head, or be it for any other cause. Up to about a hundred years ago, the physician was faced with a cruel decision, because the life of the mother competed with that of the infant. Caesarean section, which might save the infant, spelled almost certain death for the mother, or, from about the eighteenth century to the later nineteenth, involved at least a very high risk. Should he sacrifice the mother for the slim chance of saving the child? Should he save the mother at the expense of the infant, which, if not already dead, would be killed in the process of diminishing its size? Which life demanded more respect? Or was there a higher law that forbade the sacrifice of either and thereby all but ensured the death of both?

It might be argued that the decision was already made when the physician decided for or against abortion and that Soranus, who admitted performing therapeutic abortion, was consistent in teaching the destruction of the infant, with the explanation, "even if one loses the infant, it is still necessary to take care of the mother."[24] But some early Christian authors saw the matter in a different light. Tertullian, the great patristic writer of the third century, decried abortion as murder; yet he condoned killing the infant, lest it become "a murderer of the mother."[25] I am unable to say how far the voice of Tertullian and the similar voices of Augustine and Eusebius, countenancing destruction of the unborn child as a last resort, were heeded, or whether they were lost in the general theological condemnation of abortion and surgical destruction (craniotomy, insertion of hooks, embryotomy) said to have prevailed during the Middle Ages.[26]

The anguish of the physician is well described by an author of the late sixteenth century. In a case of difficult labor, and if in doubt whether the child was still alive or dead, "what should Christian physicians do and what plan should they follow? For if they abandon the patient without help, they will be accused of being inhuman; if, however, they rashly have recourse to manual operation and to pulling with instruments and, to save the woman, kill the fetus that, perchance still alive, has not yet been baptized, they will burden their own conscience, since evil things should never be done that good may result. They will have to account for their deed to the Highest." Our author then describes what he does when "upon the urging of Christian piety," though "somewhat reluctantly," he has to deal with such a case. If everything seems all right, "having implored the help of almighty God, I begin the work with alacrity and usually bring it to a successful end. But if the female parts . . . show considerable narrowness, I deem it better to take honest flight and to refrain from the task than to take such grave risks, all the more if the woman is of a weak constitution."[27]

In the early nineteenth century, British obstetricians charged that Caesarean section was performed more frequently on the Catholic Continent than in England, because of the willingness to risk the mother's life rather than leave the infant unbaptized.[28] But in England, where the sacrifice of the infant was deemed preferable, the decision pro or con was equally based on moral rather than strictly medical grounds. "Where are the circumstances," an opponent of Caesarean section asked, "that can ever warrant the certain endangerment, nay, often the more probable sacrifice, of a mother's life for the chance—and be it remembered it is nothing more—of preserving that of her child? How few of the children that 'have been ripped from their mother's belly like the Thane of Cawdor' have been reared?"[29] But the alternative —namely, killing the child—was condemned with equally strong and plastic arguments. "Assuredly no man would consider himself justified, on any plea whatsoever, in perforating, and breaking down with a pointed iron instrument, the skull of a living child an hour after birth, and subsequently scooping out its brain. But is the crime less when perpetrated an hour before birth?"[30]

Before the advent of safe Caesarean section and other very modern techniques, the dilemma was not solvable from inside the medical profession. The obstetrician who was an opponent of abortion might yet feel compelled to save his patient, rather than watch her die. In its elementary form the dilemma was inherent in the Hippocratic Oath, which forbade the physician to give a remedy causing the premature death of the fetus but also charged him with the welfare of the patient—that is, the mother.

5.

"Respect for life" has proved ambiguous in the history of medicine as practice. It proves no less ambiguous in the history of medicine as discipline, and in the history of the relationship between the two. The practice of medicine rests on respect for the patient, or a particular group of patients. The physician is responsible for this particular life, or these particular lives. Since all healing is based on some kind of knowledge, the cultivation of such knowledge is part of medicine, and thus human anatomy, physiology, and pathology, as well as clinical observation, are *medical* sciences. As a scientist, the physician also deals with human life, but in a general, abstract form, not with the particular life of this or that patient. The medical scientist determines the boundaries between life and death. In our time, this task has led to important redefinitions. Long ago, the heart was defined as the *ultimum moriens,* the organ that died last. Early in our century, experiments showed that the isolated and refrigerated hearts of mammals could be revived after nearly two days.[31] The brain showed no such endurance, though its death, too, entailed the death of the whole organism. If the brain was made the indicator of life or death, a person in whom it had ceased to function might be pronounced dead and the as-yet-living heart be transplanted to another individual. This is a well-known dramatic example of how science redefines human life and death biologically, leaving the legal definition to the lawyer. It shows the near-miraculous achievements of medical science within the last hundred years, since the recognition of Louis Pasteur's germ theory of infectious disease and Lister's application of it in surgery. Pasteur was a chemist, not a physician, and since his time, many scientists without medical degrees have worked in the field of medical research. The researcher for a serum or a drug that will eradicate a disease does not have to think of sick individuals. The geneticist who cautions against certain techniques of constructing DNA (deoxyribonucleic acid) molecules, the carriers of inheritance, has in mind dangers that threaten mankind.[32]

All this sounds very modern, and so it is, as long as our attention rests on scientific progress and technical achievement. But the underlying principle is very old. When medical scientists who lived in the third century B.C. were blamed for having conducted their research on criminals condemned to die, their followers defended them and maintained that it was not cruel "that in the execution of criminals, and but a few of them, we should seek remedies for innocent people of all future ages."[33] In other words, the physician's respect for life and the scientist's respect for human life in general can clash.

Since the middle of the last century, medical research and science have inclined toward the exact sciences, so that heredity is seen as a chapter in the chemistry of macromolecules, the brain as the likeness of a computer, and metabolism as a series of enzyme reactions. The old simile of the body as a machine seems irresistible, and many biologists and physicians think of life as reducible to the laws of physics and chemistry. A good physician must have good scientific training, yet what kind of respect can he be expected to have for the life of his patient if he sees in him nothing but a machine? Is the respect which a physician owes his patient the same kind of respect a mechanic may have for an expensive car? The question has been denied so often, or rather, becoming a "mere" mechanic has been held up so often as an undesirable development for the physician, that we can take a negative answer for granted. The kind of respect we have depends on the subject we are dealing with, and if we deny that man and machine demand the same respect, we imply a difference between man and machine, even if we accept reductionism in biology. The physician who has to alleviate pain deals with a feeling machine, and he has to take into account that, not only should this machine function in human society, but it can express its wishes and decide how it wants to function. The auto mechanic will consult the wishes of the owner of the car. But man owns himself; the physician must be guided by what the patient can do and wants to do in a social, cultural, and intellectual milieu.

Our analysis will sound less abstract if we translate it into the language of health and disease. Disease is undesirable: it is "bad life." There are degrees in the severity of disease, from impairments of *joie de vivre* and social functioning, through an impairment of vegetative and animal functions, to a threat to life itself. The evaluation of a disease goes beyond biology. A stroke incapacitating a man's power of movement can have greater consequences in a society of peasants and craftsmen than in a society of white-collar workers. On the other hand, a stroke that leads to dyslexia, a difficulty with reading, is disastrous for an intellectual, whereas it may go unnoticed among illiterates. Biologically speaking, both are lesions of the brain, varying in extent and localization. Health—or "good life"—also has its gradations, from excellent to bearable, and mere absence of disease is no longer considered synonymous with health. The World Health Organization has gone so far as to identify health with "a state of complete physical, mental, and social well-being."[34] Surely, this extends beyond biological values.

It was a physician, La Mettrie, who insisted that man was nothing but a machine. But as long as the physician remembers the situation of the human being for whom he is responsible, his metabiological beliefs are of secondary importance. Responsibility in practical medicine requires both scientific detachment and a sense of duty to maintain the patient in the best possible condition.

6.

Having allowed us to proceed so far, the devil's advocate may no longer be able to restrain himself. "You speak of respect for life in medicine, of responsibility and of duty," he says. "The layman, the patient, expects them, but the doctors do not live up to these expectations. You have bored us with antiquity; well, let me quote Martial, who said of an eye doctor turned gladiator: 'As a physician you did what you are now doing as a gladiator!'[35] Surely, a gladiator is not a respecter of life! You have talked of the pious medieval doctor; well, the Middle Ages saw through him and coined the adage: *'Dat Galenus opes'* (Galen gives riches). The soaring costs of medical care speak a clear language. And as to modern times, Molière unmasked the arrogance of a profession that thinks to rule over life and death. What did Dr. Purgon tell the patient when his authority was questioned?"

I have to tell you that I abandon you to your bad constitution, to the distemper of your bowels, to the corruption of your blood, to the acrimony of your bile, and to the feculence of your humors. And I wish that before four days have passed you may be in an incurable state . . . that you fall sick of bradypepsia . . . go from bradypepsia to dyspepsia . . . from dyspepsia to apepsia . . . from apepsia to lientery . . . from lientery to dysentery . . . from dysentery to dropsy . . . from dropsy to the loss of life to which your folly has led you![36]

"These are the true, unconscious thoughts of the doctors! Sigmund Freud could not have expressed it better—if only he had not been a doctor himself!"

Get thee hence, Satan! Such scurrilous remarks must not be dignified by any reply! Like most critics, the devil's advocate attacks physicians, not their art and science. Medicine can as little be judged by the behavior of some of its least admirable adepts as the Christian, Jewish, and Mohammedan religions can be judged by the behavior of some of the least admirable of their faithful followers.

But the devil's advocate is not silenced quite so easily. "If medicine really had respect for life," he continues, "it would demand that all life be respected, not only that of this or that patient, or of mankind in the abstract. It would demand that the death penalty be abolished, that all wars be ended, and that poverty cease to be a cause of disease and of death and hinder the patient's complete physical, mental, and social well-being. The defense that individual physicians must not be mistaken for medicine will not protect us here. On the contrary, some physicians have opposed the death penalty, have been pacifists, and have striven for social reform. But medicine as an art and science has not."

What have we to say to all this?

7.

Medicine does not deal with life per se; this is the biologist's concern. To physicians, "respect for life" has meant "respect for human life." Medicine has not stood for vegetarianism, and animals have been sacrificed in experiments aimed at saving or improving human life. Respect for life in medicine has, moreover, revealed itself as a complex and paradoxical idea, not free from contradictions. Medicine is silent about the meaning of the life for which it claims respect. Strictly speaking, medicine is not a person and can neither stand for something nor claim anything. "Standing for" and "claiming" are no more than convenient abbreviations, helpful in exploring how far respect for life is necessary in the practice and discipline of healing.

The meaning of life does not have to enter into medical thought. The separation of medicine and philosophy has been attributed to Hippocrates. Before him, our ancient source relates, "the curing of diseases and the contemplation of the nature of things" were in the same hands, because medical knowledge was needed, "especially by those whose bodily strength had become weakened by quiet thinking and watching by night."[37] Medicine is very much concerned with whether a patient can live, or will have to die. But in its metaphysical sense, "to be or not to be" is not a medical question. In dealing with suicide, the medical man is likely to ask what made life seem worthless; he is not likely to ponder the value of life. The paradoxical nature of the situation has revealed itself in the problem of euthanasia. Even if the patient's life is reduced to a state of vegetation, medical tradition —and, since the Middle Ages, the law as well—binds the medical man to respect this life. But medical tradition does not tell him *why* such a life should be protected and maintained, nor does it make the life of a saint more worthy of respect than the life of a sinner.

Medical respect for life exists in a void, and human nature, as well as external nature, abhors a void. Historically speaking, the void has been filled in two different ways. The one way we already encountered in various examples, in which demands pressed on medicine from outside. What presses from outside can also be an answer requested from inside on grounds of religion, philosophy, or sociopolitical ideologies. Even the Hippocratic Oath probably had a religious and philosophical background. Then Stoic ideas of philanthropy entered medicine.[38] The monotheistic religions made charity a duty, and made abortion, suicide, and euthanasia sins. God had given life, and man must not interfere with His purpose. In more modern times, work has been seen as a social and religious duty—witness Paracelsus, the contemporary of Luther, who urged physicians to search incessantly for remedies to cure diseases deemed incurable. Paracelsus's fame rested largely on his use of chemical processes to extract from drugs the potencies active against disease.[39] This chemotherapeutic notion, developed by Ehrlich into the concept of "magic bullets" killing infectious organisms, is still popular, and it fits in with our emphasis on work as necessity and duty. Potent drugs can attack man's disease, enabling him to carry on with his work and habit of life. There are even those who let cocktails and tranquilizers take care of the stress of a life that is allowed to remain as stressful as before. Life has many headaches. Take aspirin, and life will be free of all headaches!

With the awakening of the Western social conscience toward the end of the eighteenth century, not only were ideas of social reform accepted, but they were often even advocated by physicians. The revolutionary period of 1848 was a culminating point. As Erwin H. Ackerknecht has shown, medical science was believed to be the science that yielded the knowledge of man fundamental for all social sciences, and the physician was the natural advocate of the poor.[40] After the revolutionary fever subsided, these ideas lost much of their hold on physicians, but they have come back to the fore again today in discussions over health insurance and the promotion of health. Ideas of equality that spring from political and social ideologies thus urge that respect for life must be equal respect for everybody's life. If accepted or rejected with sufficient force, they make the physician turn to politics.

The other way of filling the void is to make health and life the *summum bonum,* not by explicit philosophy, but by letting respect for life operate without regard for other values that make life only a means to different ends. Health became a goal in itself in ancient, so-called dietetic medicine, which regulated man's entire life.[41] Health was thought of as a precarious balance of the body constituents. The slightest mistake in food and drink, exercise and rest, even in the sphere of emotions, could lead to illness. A man rich enough and with sufficient leisure could protect himself by perpetual medical surveillance. Of course, he had to lead the life of a hypochondriac, hypochondria being a disease to which those who live for the sake of their health are prone.

In its pure form, dietetic medicine flourished in Hellenistic Greece. The Romans had other things to do than to give themselves up to a life dedicated to their health: they were reminded by Vergil that through their empire they were supposed to rule the nations. But dietetic medicine is more than a historical episode. It represents an idea ever-inherent in medicine; the temptation is great to divide mankind into two categories of people: physicians and patients. And physicians are not the only ones to be tempted to do this. In reality, most of us live in a state of compromise. We believe in values beyond health, yet we also sometimes forget them and respect our lives more than anything else. Physicians and patients know how difficult it is to find the proper compromise.

"To be or not to be" is not a medical question, because once a person has entered medicine, he or she has already voted for being and has assumed respect for life as a responsibility and a duty. But different people have chosen the profession of medicine for different reasons, some lofty and some not so lofty. Respect for life is a necessary condition for being a physician; it is not a necessary motive for entering medicine. The question of how deeply respect for life must be felt, as long as responsibility and duty are not shirked, must be left open. Isn't this an austere, formalistic, concept of respect for life in medicine, closer to Kant's categorical imperative than to the pulsating life and warm devotion of many physicians? Albert Schweitzer taught and showed what reverence for life could and should be. Indeed, *Ehrfurcht vor dem Leben* became a focal point of Schweitzer's philosophy. "The ethic of reverence for life," he wrote, "thus includes all that can be designated as love, devotion, compassion, sharing of joy and of aspirations."[42] Reverence *(Ehrfurcht)* is more than respect *(Achtung)*. Whatever the semantic subtleties, we must not forget that Schweitzer was a theologian and a philosopher before he added medicine to his qualifications. Those ideas came to him in his striving for a philosophy of civilization, though they may, of course, have been reinforced by his medical activities in Africa. The philosopher will ponder the ethics of respect for life and its manifold meanings, and his speculations will go beyond its role in medicine.

Lest we be disappointed with the merely regulative nature of the idea in medicine, let us remember that respect for life does not exhaust the ethical foundation of medicine. Healing in the broadest sense goes beyond respect for life. Scribonius Largus said that physicians lacking in humanity and compassion were detested by men and gods. Paracelsus warned the doctors that they would fail if they lacked compassion and love.

If I may briefly step out of my role as historian, I would like to hope that a good physician will not only show respect for life but also feel it. Otherwise, he may not only easily become entangled in such snares as any inhumane regime may have ready for him, but may fail, under any regime, to satisfy the human needs of the sick.

NOTES

1. *World Medical Journal* 11 (1964): 356G. The declaration can also be found in many earlier volumes of that journal.

2. Quoted from the English translation by Ludwig Edelstein, *The Hippocratic Oath*, reprinted in *Ancient Medicine: Selected Papers of Ludwig Edelstein*, ed. Owsei Temkin and C. Lilian Temkin (Baltimore: The Johns Hopkins Press, 1967), p. 6.

3. *Soranus' Gynecology*, trans. by Owsei Temkin with the assistance of Nicholson J. Eastman, Ludwig Edelstein, and Alan F. Guttmacher (Baltimore: The Johns Hopkins Press, 1956), p. 63 (book 1, chap. 19).

4. Scribonius Largus, *Conpositiones*, ed. Georg Helmreich (Leipzig: Teubner, 1887), preface (pp. 2,27-3,2). In Karl Deichgräber's edition of the preface, *Professio medici: Zum Vorwort des Scribonius Largus* (Wiesbaden: Franz Steiner, 1950, for Akademie der Wissenschaften und der Literatur, Mainz [Abhandlungen der geistes- und sozialwissenschaftlichen Klasse, 1950, no. 9], pp. 875-79) the text of this passage is identical.

5. For the Greek text, see W. H. S. Jones's edition of *Hippocrates*, vol. 4, p. 98, in the Loeb Classical Library. My translation differs somewhat from that of Jones.

6. Galen, *In Hippocratis Aphorismos commentarii* 1 in *Opera omnia*, ed. Carl Gottlob Kühn (Leipzig: Cnobloch, 1821-33), 17B: 353,12-354,4.

7. Apuleius, *Metamorphoses* 10. 9-12. I have used *Apuleius, Metamorphosen oder Der goldene Esel*, Latin and German by Rudolf Helm, 6th ed., by Werner Krenkel (Berlin: Akademie-Verlag, 1970), pp. 330-33.

8. *Metamorphoses* 10. 9; p. 330,4-6. Helm, p. 331, translates the difficult *veterno* by *langwierig*.

9. *Metamorphoses* 10. 11; pp. 330,34-332,1.

10. Darrel W. Amundsen, "Romanticizing the ancient medical profession: the characterization of the physician in the Graeco-Roman novel," *Bull. Hist. Med.* 48 (1974): 320-37 (see pp. 323, 325).

11. *Epistulae* 5, ed. E. Littré, *Oeuvres complètes d'Hippocrate* 9 (Paris: Baillière et Fils, 1861); 316-18. In spite of the word *themis*, I cannot follow Deichgräber, *op. cit.* (n. 4 above) p. 857, who sees a religious element in Hippocrates's refusal. The letters indicate that, apart from his patriotic reasons,

Hippocrates objects to the imputation of being mercenary. For Hippocrates's patriotism, see Edelstein, "Hippokrates," in Pauly-Wissowa, *Real-Encyclopädie,* Supplement vol. 6 (1935), cols. 1300-1301.

12. Even where not put in quotation marks, the paraphrase follows the wording of the text rather closely. Deichgräber's (see above, n. 4) edition of the passage, p. 876,29-37, which I have accepted, differs slightly from that of Helmreich (see above, n. 4), p. 2,16-26, but it seems to correspond more closely to my interpretation, which I have tried to bring out by rearranging the sequence of the arguments. See also Deichgräber, p. 867. Edelstein, "The professional ethics of the Greek physician," reprinted in *Ancient Medicine* (see above, n. 2), pp. 319-48, on p. 339 translates the passage *qui sacramento medicinae legitime est obligatus* (ed. Helmreich, p. 2,20-21; Deichgräber, p. 876,32-33) by "bound in lawful obedience to medicine by his military oath." The assumption of a special oath for army surgeons seems unwarranted to me.

13. *Epistulae* 11; ed. Littré, vol. 9, p. 328,14.

14. Cf. Edelstein, "The professional ethics," *Ancient Medicine,* pp. 340, 342 (n. 12 above), and Deichgräber, *op. cit.* (n. 4 above) p. 867. Scribonius, in speaking of compassion *(misericordia)* and humanity *(humanitas),* states the motives that lead him to respect the life of friend and foe alike. The Hippocratic Oath makes no reference to wealth and rank of patients, and the Hippocratic writings admonish the physician "to help, or at least to do no harm" *(Epidemics* 1. 11; Jones's translation, vol. 1, p. 165, of the Loeb edition), which corresponds to Scribonius Largus, ed. Helmreich, p. 3,5 (ed. Deichgräber, p. 876,44f.): "for medicine is the science of healing, not of harming." The whole complex of questions here discussed has been commented on by Fridolf Kudlien, "Medical ethics and popular ethics in Greece and Rome," *Clio medica* 5 (1970): 91-121 (especially pp. 91-96). I cannot, however, agree that the dilemma between physician and good citizen existed for the peripatetic Hippocratic physician as it existed for the Roman Scribonius Largus.

15. For instance, Jacme d'Agramont at the beginning of his *Regiment de preservacio a epidemia o pestilencia e mortaldats,* trans. by M. L. Duran-Reynals and C.-E. A. Winslow, *Bull. Hist. Med.* 23 (1949): 57-89.

16. "The Principles of Medical Ethics of the American Medical Association" (adopted in 1912), chap. 3, sec. 1: "Physicians, as good citizens and because their professional training specially qualifies them to render their service, should give advice concerning the public health of the community," quoted from the reprint in Chauncey D. Leake, ed., *Percival's Medical Ethics* (Baltimore: Williams and Wilkins, 1927, p. 269).

17. The passage occurs in the letter of Arsenius to Nepotian, and is here quoted from Loren C. MacKinney, "Medical ethics and etiquette in the early middle ages: the persistence of Hippocratic ideals," *Bull. Hist. Med.* 26 (1952): 1-31 (see p. 12).

18. See Paul Diepgen, *Die Theologie und der ärztliche Stand* (Berlin-Grunewald: Walter Rothschild, 1922), pp. 48 ff.

19. *De adventu medici ad aegrotum,* in Salvatore De Renzi, *Collectio Salernitana* 2 (Naples: Filiatre-Sebezio, 1853); 74-80 (see p. 74). See also Diepgen, *loc. cit.* (n. 18 above).

20. Article "Prognostic" in *Encyclopédie ou Dictionnaire raisonné des sciences, des arts et des métiers*, (new ed.) 27 (Geneva: Pellet, 1778); 524-25 (see p. 524).

21. Percival, *Medical Ethics*, chap. 2, art. 3; quoted from the reprint by Chauncey D. Leake (see above, n. 16), p. 91.

22. "Code of Ethics of the American Medical Association" (as adopted 1847 and published 1848), chap. 1, art. 4; quoted from the reprint by Chauncey D. Leake (see above, n. 16), pp. 220 ff.

23. Galen, *In Hippocratis Epidemiarum Commentaria* 4. 10; ed. Ernst Wenkebach and Franz Pfaff, *Corpus Medicorum Graecorum* 5. 10,2,2; reprinted Berlin: Academia Litterarum, 1956, p. 203. For commentary see Karl Deichgräber, *Medicus gratiosus: Untersuchung zu einem griechischen Arztbild* (Wiesbaden: Franz Steiner, 1970, for Akademie der Wissenschaften und der Literatur, Mainz [Abhandlungen der geistes- und sozialwissenschaftlichen Klasse, 1970, no. 3], p. 33 (223).

24. Soranus, *op. cit.* (n. 3 above), p. 189 (book 4, chap. 3, art. 9).

25. Tertullian, *De anima* 25. 4-6; ed. J. H. Waszink (Amsterdam: Meulenhoff 1947), pp. 36, 326. Cf. Franz Joseph Dölger, "Das Lebensrecht des ungeborenen Kindes und die Fruchtabtreibung in der Bewertung der heidnischen und christl chen Antike," *Antike und Christentum* 4 (1934): 1-61 (see pp. 42, 49); also Ru Hähnel, "Der künstliche Abortus im Altertum," *Sudhoffs Archiv* 29 (193 224-55.

26. For Augustine and Eusebius see Dölger, *op. cit.* (fn. 25), pp. 44-49, 280 Tertullian's reluctant acceptance of surgical destruction rested on the hu right (here the mother's) to turn against anybody threatening one's God-given a principle for which later theologians (see below, n. 28) cited Saint Th Aquinas "and most theologians." It should, however, not be overlooked Tertullian's excuse of the physician's practice is merely part of his argume the fetus's possessing a soul. In the question of destruction, as well as of b in the womb, much casuistry seems to have been involved, for which nn. 27 cite examples and for which articles in vol. 1, pp. 331-39, and vol. 3, pp. 1 *The Casuist* (New York: Wagner, 1906 and 1910) (acquaintance with whi to the courtesy of Mr. Stephen M. Winters) may also be consulted.

27. Julius Caesar Arantius, *Anatomicae observationes*, chap. 39 in *De foetu liber*, 3d ed. (Venice: Jacob Brechtanus, 1587), pp. 106 ff. Cf. Fasbender, *Geschichte der Geburtshilfe* (Jena: Gustav Fischer, 1906), François Mauriceau *(Traité des maladies des femmes grosses et de cell accouchées*, 4th ed. [Paris: Laurent d'Houry, 1694], pp. 295 ff.) seems t one of the earliest modern obstetricians to admit practicing embry living child, if it prevented the mother's certain death. (See also Fasbe n. 1). Mauriceau's English translator, Hugh Chamberlen *(The Diseas with Child and in Child-Bed*, [London: Bell, 1710]), remarks in his p "In the 17th chapter of the second Book, my Author justifies the fa in the Head of a Child that comes right, and yet because of some Disproportion cannot pass; which I confess has been and is yet the most expert Artists in Midwifery not only in England, but throu and has much caused the Report, That where a Man [i.e., an obst one or both must necessarily die; and is the reason for forbearing

Child is dead, or the Mother dying." This suggests that killing the child to save the mother was a more widespread practice than the literature indicates; See also below, n. 28.

28. J. H. Young, *Caesarean Section: The History and Development of the Operation from Earliest Times* (London: Lewis and Co., 1944), pp. 90 ff. In this connection (cf. Young, pp. 39-40), an opinion by the theologians of the Sorbonne on the advisability of Caesarean section is of interest. The matter is to be found in the French translation (with additions) by Jacques-Jean Bruier d'Ablaincourt of Deventer's work, in which craniotomy was taught. This French edition (*Observations importantes sur le manuel des accouchemens, traduite du Latin de M. Henry de Deventer*, première partie, [Paris: Giffart, 1734]) contains a chapter on Caesarean section (pp. 345-57) followed by a memoir requesting an opinion from the doctors of theology of the University of Paris (pp. 357-59) regarding the alternative of embryotomy versus Caesarean section, together with the possibility of baptizing the unborn child. The reply (pp. 359-65) focused on Caesarean section, so that the alternative, embryotomy, was implied rather than treated explicitly. Caesarean section was to be performed if there was hope of saving both mother and child. It was not allowed if it would lead to the mother's certain death, for this would be homicide, and it was not permissible "to do evil in order to achieve good" (i.e., the infant's baptism). Caesarean section was allowed, even if its success was doubtful, if otherwise both mother and child faced certain death. If, however, the operation would save only mother or child without well-founded hope for both, then mere justice allowed the "use of every proper means" to save the mother's life, even "exposing the child to certain death." However, "charity demands that the mother prefer the salvation of her child to her own life, if the infant's baptism can be procured only at the expense of her death." Quite apart from the insistence that the mother choose charity, did "every proper means" imply embryotomy (including craniotomy)?

The Sorbonne was reasonably clear on Caesarean section, but not equally so on embryotomy of the living child, be it that it was taken for granted, be it that a clear answer was shunned. Nevertheless, this decision of 1733 did not categorically exclude the practice of Mauriceau and other surgeons. The Sorbonne viewed the chances of successful Caesarean section relatively optimistically. The theological attitude against embryotomy hardened in the nineteenth century, when the chances of a woman surviving a Caesarean section greatly improved (see the article on "abortion" in *The Catholic Encyclopedia* 1 [New York: Universal Knowledge Foundation, 1907]: 47 ff., and the *Casuist* 3; 178-81).

29. Anonymous reviewer of 1843, cited by Young, ibid. p. 79. The reviewer claimed that Caesarean section was frequently performed on the Continent because the patients there (especially in France), "at least those amongst the poorer classes, seem to be regarded, not so much as fellow creatures that have the same hopes and desires as ourselves, but rather as objects, so to speak, of natural history, which the learned doctor has to speculate and experiment upon." C. Lilian Temkin has drawn my attention to a mistake in the quotation from Shakespeare's *Macbeth* (act 5, scene 7): Not the Thane of Cawdor—i.e., Macbeth —but "Macduff was from his mother's womb untimely ripp'd."

30. *The Obstetric Memoirs and Contributions of James Y. Simpson*, ed. W. O. Priestley and Horatio R. Storer, 2 vols. (Philadelphia: Lippincott, 1855-56), vol. 1, . 540. The section of the article in which the quoted passage appears had

previously been published in the *Edinburgh Monthly Journal of Medical Science*, 1852, and was, therefore, not intended for laymen.

31. A. Kuliabko, "Studien über die Wiederbelebung des Herzens," *Pflügers Archiv* 90 (1902): 461–71.

32. See the report of Nicholas Wade in *Science* 187 (1975): 931–35.

33. Celsus, *De Medicina*, prooemium 26; translation by W. G. Spencer in the edition of the Loeb Classical Library, vol. 1, p. 15.

34. "Constitution of the World Health Organization," *Chronicle of the World Health Organization* 1 (1947): 29.

35. Martial, *Epigrams* 8. 74.

36. *Le malade imaginaire*, act 3, scene 5. The interjections by the other people in the scene have been omitted.

37. Celsus, *De medicina*, prooemium 6–7; Spencer's translation (see above, n. 33), vol. 1, p. 5.

38. See Edelstein, "The professional ethics of the Greek physician" (see above, n. 12), pp. 329 ff.

39. See Owsei Temkin, *The Falling Sickness*, 2d ed. (Baltimore: The Johns Hopkins Press, 1971), pp. 170–72.

40. Erwin H. Ackerknecht, *Rudolf Virchow: Doctor, Statesman, Anthropologist* (Madison: University of Wisconsin Press, 1953), pp. 44–46

41. This discussion of ancient dietetics is based on Ludwig Edelstein, "The dietetics of Antiquity," in *Ancient Medicine* (above, n. 12), pp. 303–16. This article had originally appeared in German in 1931.

42. Albert Schweitzer, *Aus meinem Leben und Denken* (Hamburg: Richard Meiner, 1954), p. 134. Cf. the English translation by C. T. Campion, *Out of My Life and Thought* (New York: Holt, 1949), p. 159.

TWO

William K. Frankena

THE ETHICS OF RESPECT
FOR LIFE

Expressions like "respect for life," "reverence for life," and "the sanctity of life" have a currency today they never had before. Outside of Schweitzer, whose writings are recent, they occur mainly in discussions of a family of topics now very much in both the public and the philosophical eyes, topics grouped together under such headings as "medical ethics," "bioethics," "environmental ethics," or "ecoethics." They serve, somewhat vaguely and ambiguously, to identify a concept or group of concepts—or rather, a doctrine or group of doctrines—that are central in those discussions. The point is that many of those who take conservative positions on the matters referred to are appealing to what they call "respect for life," "the sanctity of life," etc., and regard their opponents as denying this. As one of them put it on television not long ago: "Until recently we believed life to be a sacred value, now we do not." My part in this symposium is to say something about this doctrine from a philosophical point of view, either historically or systematically, and I propose to be partly historical and partly systematic, since my interests run both ways and may be combined. What I hope to do is to provide some help in our thinking on relevant topics. At present our thinking about them is a kind of potpourri of ideas and theses partly

24

historical and partly logical or philosophical, and I shall begin by introducing some distinctions and definitions that seem to me necessary for understanding and discussing them.

1.

We are talking about "respect (or reverence) for life" and "sanctity of life." These two and similar phrases recur in relevant discussions, and I shall use them more or less interchangeably. If one has respect for life, one believes life has sanctity, and vice versa. If one believes we should respect life, one believes in the sanctity of life, and vice versa. But now, as Socrates might ask, what does the word "life" refer to in this context? In bioethical discussions, it is usually used to refer to human life, but, of course, it may also be used to refer to life in general, life of all kinds, and is so used in ecoethical discussions, which are part of what we are interested in here. Accordingly, I shall divide our subject into two parts: the topic of respect for human life, or life in human form, and that of respect for life as such or life in all its forms; and I shall call the latter *comprehensive* respect for life and the former *noncomprehensive* respect for life. Let us take the former—respect for human life—first.

Even then the denotation of "life" is not entirely fixed, and concern for life may mean concern for each individual life or concern for the life of the human species. Tennyson recognized this when he said of Nature (felicitously but unhappily),

> So careful of the type she seems,
> So careless of the single life . . .[1]

Between these two kinds of concern for life, there would also be concern for the life of one's lineage and of one's tribe or race. Here I shall be interested primarily in concern for the individual life,

1. Notes may be found on pp. 60-62.

since this seems to be what is central in bioethics, but I shall also refer on occasion to the life of the species, etc. Even then—in the case of the individual—we can speak of his bodily or physical life and of his mental life, and in some views the latter may have begun before the former and go on longer, perhaps even eternally, either in a disembodied way or in another body or a resurrected one. I shall take it that what is primarily in question here is the former, and so ordinarily mean by "life" the sort of bodily thing possessed by us between conception or birth and death. It is clearly life of this sort that is prevented, taken, etc. in abortion, contraception, euthanasia, suicide, and the like.

There have been many metaphysical views about what human life in this sense involves—naturalism, supernaturalism, dualism, materialism, idealism, epiphenomenalism, transmigrationism, behaviorism, and the identity theory. Some of these views have been used to support, and others to refute, a belief in the sanctity of human life. I shall, however, refer to them only occasionally, my general feeling being that such metaphysical positions are less relevant to our ethical issues than is often thought. I am not sure that any of them are incompatible with a belief in the sanctity of human life, except perhaps those, if any, that deny the existence of consciousness in human beings, or of such experiences as pleasure, pain, happiness, suffering, hope, and despair.

We must make more distinctions in the meaning of "life" at this point. First, we must distinguish between respect for human *life* in the biological sense just defined—that is, respect for existence as a living human organism—and respect for human individuality or personality. I say this because some writers, for example, Hans Jonas,[2] seem to equate the sanctity of human life and the sanctity of human individuality or personality. But being an individual or person and having personality include much more than being alive, and one may have respect for individuality, personhood, or personality without having respect for life as such, and vice versa. Somewhat more carefully, Edward Shils says that "three forms of life" are referred to in "the postulate of the sanctity of human life": the life of the lineage, already referred to, the life of the human organism, which I am taking as central, and the life of the individual as an individual "possessing consciousness of itself as an agent and patient both in the past and the present" and the like. "The sanctity of the individual," he says, "is a variant form of the sanctity of life." Thus he regards concern about what he calls "contrived intervention" as concern for the sanctity of life, including concern not only about abortion and artificial inovulation but also about genetic engineering, medical modification of personality qualities, and "intervention . . . into the islands of privacy which surround individuality."[3] This is, explicitly or implicitly, a rather common view, but it does involve giving a very extended sense to the terms "life" and "respect for life" and covers up the fact that abortion and personality modification, euthanasia and invasion of individuality, are very different things, one involving the taking of what is usually called "life" and the other not. It seems to me better to notice clearly and to underline this difference and to speak of concern for life in one case and for individuality or personality in the other. Not all the moral problems of medicine are questions about the sanctity of life; and some of the rights discussed go beyond those recognized in respect for life, at least in the sense in which I mean to understand it here.[4] It still may be, of course, that human life should be respected, only or partly, *because* it is a seat for individuality or personality, but that is another matter.

In a somewhat similar way, we must distinguish concern about *quantity* of life in the sense of concern about the length of an individual's life or about the number of individual lives (such as is involved in discussions of abortion, suicide, contraception, war, human sacrifice, and population control), from concern for the *quality* of life and for improving it (such as we hear so much about in discussions of ecology and the environment). Concern for the quality of life is not strictly concern for life but for something else—goodness of life, freedom of life, etc. One may seek to reduce differences in the quality of life to differences in quantity, as Herbert Spencer tried to do by talking about differences in the "breadth" or fullness of life, and then defining this in terms of the quantity of change packed into a given time, but this is not very convincing, as Spencer himself in effect admits when he says his view presupposes that conduct which promotes "the greatest totality of life" also promotes pleasure or happiness.[5]

2.

Now that we are reasonably clear what respect for human life is respect *for*, namely (roughly) bodily life, what *is* respect for life? I assume that the desire to live is primitive in man—that, although they may come to reject life and risk it every day, people do normally want to go on living. If altruistic, they may also desire that others live longer and that there be more of them. But such love of life and of the living is not *respect* for life; in Kant's terms it is "pathological," for it does not include any normative or value judgment about its object as such. To respect life is to believe in the "sanctity" of life, and this entails making some kind of normative or value judgment about it, not just feeling or acting in a certain way toward it.[6] Desiring or loving something does not by itself include making any such judgment; though it may generate such a judgment, that judgment is not simply an articulation or report of mere desire or love.[7] Well, what kind of a normative or value judgment is involved in respect for life? It might be a judgment of admiration, of aesthetic appreciation, or of cognitive curiosity—of what C. I. Lewis called "inherent value"[8]—like "Life is beautiful." I think we generally do have such aesthetic or cognitive interests in contemplating life; even if we do not find it all admirable or beautiful, we do tend to find it interesting. And, indeed, in the discussions relevant here, there do sometimes appear quasi-aesthetic expressions like "human dignity," "the dignity of the individual," and the "dignity" or "integrity" of human life.[9] It is then, however, usually clear that "dignity" does not have a merely aesthetic meaning, and that the concern in such contexts is not just aesthetic or contemplative, but ethical.[10] Respect here is not just a kind of admiration or curiosity; it may actually contain no admiration or curiosity at all.

It may be thought that respect for life is or includes a judgment of value that is not aesthetic but also is not moral—for example, a judgment like "Life is good," or "Life is worth living." In fact, excepting maybe Rousseau and Bret Harte, none of us believe that human life is *morally* good, for this would be to believe that there are no bad people. But it is often held that life is good or worth living in either an instrumental or an intrinsic way, though pessimists have sometimes denied this. Thus, in *The Morals of Evolution,* M. J. Savage maintained that "life . . . is worth living for itself alone," and somewhat earlier Robert Browning wrote these lines:[11]

> How good is man's life, the mere living! How fit to employ
> All the heart and the soul and the senses for ever in joy![12]

These verses make it sound as if all human life were like the beginning of *Oklahoma,* and are contradicted by what happens later in that same story, but, in any case, those who believe in the sanctity of life in our context are not holding that life is good in itself in this way; they may do so, of course, but they hold that even if or when it is not, human life still has sanctity in their sense. Indeed, it is doubtful that anyone ever really believed that "mere living" is good or worth doing in the sense of holding either that life is good in itself, no matter how it is qualified, even if it is painful and vicious, or that mere living is so, even if or when it is unconscious and contains no pleasure or pain, hope or fear, aspiration or achievement. Certainly, to assert the sanctity of life is not just to assert that it is good as a means to something else; it is true that life is, at least while we are on earth, a necessary condition of our enjoyment or achievement of value or disvalue, and because it is, perhaps we should ascribe sanctity to it, but to say it is is not necessarily to ascribe sanctity to it. Ascribing sanctity to life is not just judging that it is worth living as a means or in itself; it is more like judging that one living being should respect other living beings. So, once again, what *is* respect for human life?

Two rather different answers have to be distinguished. One is to say that human life is "sacred," "sacrosanct, " or even "holy"; the other is to say that live human beings have certain rights, that it is wrong to treat them in certain ways. These two lines of thought are often confused or conflated, but, even if the first entails the second, they should be distinguished. It seems, to me at least, that the doctrine of the sanctity of life takes these two rather different forms: a religious or protoreligious form in which it is natural to speak of respect for human life as including *awe* for it, and a more purely ethical or moral form in which it is not natural or at least not necessary to do so. The first, of course, is maintained by many religious thinkers—for example, Karl Barth, Paul Ramsey, and Hans Jonas.[13] Interestingly, however, it is also maintained by the social scientist Edward Shils, who regards it as "self-evident" that life is "sacred" and thinks that its sacredness is so basic and primitive as to be presupposed both by the religious and by the ethical beliefs in the sanctity of human life.

The source of the revulsion or apprehension [about "contrived intervention"] is deeper than the culture of Christianity . . . [in] a deeper, protoreligious "natural metaphysics." . . . The chief feature of [this] is the affirmation that life *is* sacred. It is believed to be sacred not because it is a manifestation of a transcendent creator . . . [but] because it is life. The idea of sacredness is generated by the primordial experience of being alive, of experiencing the elemental sensation of vitality and the elemental fear of its extinction. Man stands in awe before his own vitality, the vitality of his lineage and of his species. The sense of awe is the attribution and therefore the acknowledgement of sanctity . . . the transcendent sacred is a construction which the human mind itself has created to account for and to place in a necessary order the primordial experience. . . . If life were not viewed and experienced as sacred, then nothing else would be sacred. . . .

[Is] human life really sacred? I answer that it is, self-evidently. Its sacredness is the most primordial of experiences . . . the task for our generation and those immediately following is not so much the re-establishment of . . . Christianity . . . but rather the rediscovery of . . . the protoreligion, the "natural metaphysic" of the sanctity of life.[14]

The second form of the doctrine of respect for life is or at least may be held independently of religion in anything like its traditional forms. It is also possible for one to subscribe to the doctrine in both forms, without holding that the second depends on the first; it may be that Ramsey and Jonas do this—they do implicitly distinguish the religious and the moral forms of the doctrine—but they still regard the second as in some way inade-quate.[15] More typically, theologians, especially Protestant and Jewish ones, have held that the religious form of the doctrine both entails and is presupposed by the moral form. They also typically claim, as we shall see, that the moral doctrine of the sanctity of life emerged historically from the Judeo-Christian religion, and even that it would not have appeared if that religion had not entered the world.

Shils's position is interesting here, for he holds that the moral view depends on the other one, both historically and logically (if I understand him), but denies that it depends, either historically or logically, on "the culture of Christianity and its doctrine of the soul" or on any traditional religious belief or faith. I cannot try to assess his views here, though I think they should not simply be brushed off. Even if Shils is correct in his historical thesis, however, it seems certain, as we shall see, that Judeo-Christian religious beliefs did play a large role in the emergence of the moral form of respect for life. In any case, it seems to me that for us, in connection with the problems of bio- and ecoethics, the crucial form of the doctrine of the sanctity of life is the moral one, and that any religious form of the doctrine is of interest only if it is presupposed, genetically or logically, by the moral one. In short, I take respect for human life, in the sense in which we are concerned with it, to involve the making of a specifically *moral* judgment about such life (not just a value judgment of some other sort, religious or nonreligious); that is, it involves saying that certain attitudes toward or ways of treating human life (bodily life) are *morally* good or bad, right or wrong. I am supported in this by a feeling that judgments of sacredness, awesomeness, holiness, etc. are more like aesthetic ones than like moral ones, and a consequent doubt that they are presupposed by moral ones (rather than the other way around).[16]

It should be observed that since "human life has sanctity" (or "is to be respected"), in the sense in which we shall take it here, *means* that it is morally wrong to treat human life in certain ways, one cannot sensibly say that it is wrong to treat human life in these ways *because* human life has sanctity, for this will be a mere tautology.

3.

We must make even more distinctions. So far I have been arguing that we should take as central the idea of *moral* respect for *quantity* of *individual* human *bodily* life—that is, the idea that some or all acts reducing the quantity—duration or number—of such bodily life or lives are morally wrong. We must now notice, first, that such acts are of two kinds: acts of ending or shortening a human bodily life—for example, killing, suicide, and euthanasia; and acts of preventing possible human bodily life —contraception (even rhythm), sterilization, celibacy, refraining from sexual intercourse, etc. Acts of abortion will fall under either heading—under the first if fetuses are human beings, as Ramsey and others think, under the second if they are not, as still others think. By *unqualified* respect for human life (or belief in the sanctity of human life) I shall mean the view that all acts of either kind are wrong, absolutely or *ceteris paribus;* by *qualified* respect for human life, the view that some or all acts of the second sort are permissible or right but acts of the first sort are wrong, at least prima facie in Ross's sense.[17]

As was just implied, each of these views can be held in either of two ways: one may hold that the sanctity of human life is absolute in the sense that it is never overruled by other considerations —that it is always actually wrong to end or prevent a human life; or one may hold that it is not absolute—that it is always wrong presumptively, wrong *ceteris paribus,* or prima facie wrong, to shorten or prevent a human life, but not always actually or finally wrong, since other moral considerations may still make it right in certain circumstances. For example, in the famous case in which a choice must be made between killing a fetus and allowing both fetus and mother to die, the first view will choose the latter alternative, and the second the former. Both views subscribe to the sanctity of human life, but in different ways; both regard killing the fetus as wrong as such, but the second view holds that its wrongness is overridden by the fact that otherwise both fetus and mother will die, while the first view denies this. The fact that a belief in the sanctity of life can take these two forms is important to remember, for it is often assumed—by our television speaker and by Temple and Fletcher in the argument to be discussed later, for example—that those who believe in the sanctity of human life must hold that it is absolute and inviolable, and that those who hold it to be sometimes right to end a fetal or human life do not believe that it has any sanctity. Even Henry Sidgwick makes this assumption.

My final distinction may be introduced as follows. By belief in the sanctity of human life one may simply mean belief that abortion and other acts of the kinds just listed are morally wrong, either absolutely or prima facie. This seems to be what W. E. H. Lecky and Ludwig Edelstein mean in the discussions we shall review shortly. However, like Socrates, we must ask here what makes the actions listed wrong, what they have in common, and the answer must be that they are wrong because they involve the shortening or preventing of a human bodily life. Or else no respect for human bodily life as such is at issue. For example, if it is held that such acts are wrong just because they are forbidden by God, no doctrine of the sanctity of bodily life is implied, unless it is added that God forbids them qua acts of shortening or preventing such life. But even if such acts are taken to be wrong, absolutely or *ceteris paribus,* qua acts of shortening or preventing human bodily life, they may be taken to be so in different ways. If we ask what makes acts of shortening or preventing human bodily life wrong, then one answer is to say that such acts are wrong just because they are acts of ending or preventing a human bodily life. In this view (and only in this view), the sanctity of human life, absolute or presumptive, is a *basic* ethical principle, holding that we should respect human bodily life as such, because of what it is and not because of other facts about it. The other answer is to say that human bodily life is to be respected (or has sanctity) not because of what it is but because of other facts about it—such as that it is accompanied by consciousness, is a condition of intellectual or moral perfection, or is loved or valued by God. On this second view, the sanctity of human life, whether absolute or presumptive, is a *derivative* ethical principle, based on a prior principle to the effect that we should respect consciousness, seek perfection, or love what God loves. In both views, the sanctity of human physical life is maintained, but only in the first is it held to have sanctity *as such*. In other words, in the first view such life is respected *directly,* as such, or for its own sake; in the second it is respected *indirectly,* for the sake of something else—consciousness, perfection, or God. The latter view is that life has a kind of sanctity all right, but not qua life; in this sense only the first view entails a straight-out respect for *life*.

4.

These distinctions made, let us look at the history of the idea of the sanctity of human life. The television speaker quoted earlier said we used to believe that life has sanctity, but that today we do not. This statement is inaccurate: we never all believed that life had sanctity even in the moral sense, and some of us still do. What is true is that, not long ago, abortion, suicide, etc. were much more generally proscribed in Western morality and law than they now are. It is also true that they were much less proscribed in ancient times than they were more recently. Indeed, we may say that, at least until lately, there was a gradual evolution of respect for human life in the moral and legal systems of the West, if not in the actual "practice" of Western man, then at least in his "preaching," in his judgments about abortion, infanticide, human sacrifice, gladiatorial combat, murder, suicide, and war. One small sign of this is the way the use of the Hippocratic oath, so carefully studied by Edelstein, came to be an increasing part of the ethics of the medical profession, a story I will come back to. Most accounts of the development of our law and morality agree about this. The classical account is that of Lecky in his *History of European Morals* (1869), in which the expression "the sanctity of human life" was already (first?) used.

Considered as immortal beings, destined for the extremes of happiness or of misery, and united to one another by a special community of redemption, the first and most manifest duty of a Christian man was to look upon his fellowmen as sacred beings, and from this notion grew up the eminently Christian idea of the sanctity of human life . . . nature does not tell man that it is wrong to slay without provocation his fellowmen . . . it was one of the most important services of Christianity that besides quickening greatly our benevolent affections it definitely and dogmatically asserted the sinfulness of all destruction of human life as a matter of amusement, or of simple convenience, and thereby formed a new standard higher than any which then existed in the world . . . This minute and scrupulous care for human life and human virtue in the humblest form, in the slave, the gladiator, the savage, or the infant, was indeed wholly foreign to the genius of Paganism. It was produced by the Christian doctrine of the inestimable value of each immortal soul.[18]

Except for some more evolutionary writers, most historians of Western morals agree with Lecky that the rise of Judaism and even more of Christianity, had a great deal to do with the growth of the "sense of the sanctity of human life"—that there was either little or no recognition of the sanctity of life in ancient pagan culture, and that any such recognition was either generated or greatly increased by the advent of the Judaic and Christian religions, through their doctrines of creation, the nature of God, ethics, the immortality of the soul, and the hereafter. It seems to me that this general picture is approximately correct. To complete it in the same rough global way, we may say, as was indicated, that this growth of the sense of the sanctity of human life has received a considerable *échec* in recent decades, no doubt partly because of the decline and fall of the Judeo-Christian empire over our minds; but we must add that we are at the same time seeing a broadening of the notion of respect for life to include not just human or even animal life but also plant life and, indeed, all of nature—that is, of what I called comprehensive respect for life, a broadening that seems to have no special ties with the Judeo-Christian tradition (though at least some thinkers in that tradition seem to favor it) and may be mainly influenced by romanticism, evolutionism, and Indian philosophy.[19]

This rather global picture cannot be fully documented here, but some comments and points, mainly historical, must be made. (1) One can ask whether there has been a growth of the sense of the sanctity of human life even within Judaism and Christianity. I am disposed to think there was, though Lecky points out that proscriptions of some things like abortion, infanticide, and human sacrifice were part of Christianity from the very beginning, but I shall not discuss this question.

(2) More interesting is the question of the extent of the sense of the sanctity of human life in Western ancient pagan culture. In their apologetics, Judeo-Christian theologians sometimes minimize it, and it certainly is true that the Greeks and Romans (to say nothing of those they called "barbarians") had less of this sense than the Christians, judging by their attitudes to abortion, etc. But, as Georgia Harkness says, there is a kind of respect for life in every society. "In every society there appears to be an elemental reverence for life which makes the deliberate killing of

another person a punishable offense. In all societies there are exceptions . . . yet aversion to murder is probably the most universal of all moral attitudes."[20] As for abortion, etc., there was at least some disapproval of such kinds of action, and even some legal prohibition, in Greek and Roman society, as Lecky makes clear. It remains true that the idea of the sanctity of human life is far from complete even in the best pagan philosophers, if measured by their attitudes toward abortion, etc. or toward barbarians.[21]

(3) Edelstein's discussion of the Hippocratic Oath and the Pythagoreans, which has already been mentioned, is relevant here. Among other things, the oath, which he assigns to the fourth century B.C., includes the article quoted by Dr. Temkin, which expresses a strong disapproval of abortion, euthanasia, and suicide, independently of Judeo-Christian influence. Discussing this clause, Edelstein contends that it did not reflect the general view (let alone the practice) of the physicians of Greece or Rome and was not subscribed to by physicians generally until "the end of antiquity"—until Christianity arose and became dominant—and that, in fact, it was not an expression of any prevailing Greek views, and long represented "a small segment of Greek opinion."

Ancient jurisdiction did not discriminate against suicide; it did not attach any disgrace to it, provided that there was sufficient reason for such an act. And self-murder as a relief from illness was regarded as justifiable . . . in some states it was an institution duly legalized by the authorities. Nor did Greek or Roman law protect the unborn child. If, in certain cities, abortion was prosecuted, it was because the father's right to his offspring had been violated by the mother's action. Ancient religion did not proscribe suicide. It did not know of any eternal punishment for those who voluntarily ended their lives. Likewise it remained indifferent to foeticide. . . . Law and religion then left the physician free to do whatever seemed best to him.

From these considerations it follows that a specific philosophical conviction must have dictated the rules laid down in the Oath. Is it possible to determine this particular philosophy? To take the problem of suicide first: Platonists, Cynics, and Stoics can be eliminated at once. They held suicide permissible for the diseased. Some . . . even extolled such an act as the greatest triumph of men over fate. Aristotle . . . and

Epicurus [were opposed to suicide but this] did not involve moral censure. If men decided to take their lives, they were within their rights. . . . The Aristotelian and Epicurean schools condoned suicide. Later on the Aristotelians . . . under the onslaught of the Stoic attack [even] . . . withdrew their disapproval of self-murder . . . indeed among all Greek thinkers the Pythagoreans alone outlawed suicide and did so without qualification . . . the same can be asserted of the rule forbidding abortion. . . . Most of the Greek philosophers even commended abortion. For Plato, foeticide is one of the regular institutions of the ideal state . . . Aristotle reckons abortion the best procedure to keep the population within the limits which he considers essential for a well-ordered community.[22]

Edelstein then recognizes that Aristotle and later Greek philosophers held that abortion is permissible only before the fetus attains the state of "animated" life, but adds that they did not hold that animation begins at conception but somewhat later, or not until birth. Then he says, "It was different with the Pythagoreans. They held that the embryo was an animate being from the moment of conception . . . [and] could not but reject abortion unconditionally." He further contends that this article, and the oath generally, must be regarded as an expression of the Pythagorean philosophy and/or religion of the fourth century B.C., which did prohibit abortion and suicide, and in general held to a very rigoristic regimen, wishing thereby to reform both medicine and life.

I have a feeling that, to make his case for the Pythagorean origin of the oath, Edelstein slightly understates the extent to which the other ancients disapproved of abortion and suicide. Still, his general line of argument is convincing, and, while it does establish that Pythagoreanism was an exception to the usual picture described earlier, it also makes clear that Pythagoreanism was the kind of exception that helps to prove the rule envisaged in that picture. One may doubt, however, that the Pythagoreans really did regard life as having sanctity *as such*. Whether or not they did depends on their reasons for proscribing abortion and suicide. Their argument against suicide, Lecky and Edelstein agree, was "that we are all soldiers of God, placed in an appointed post of duty, which it is a rebellion against our Maker to desert,"[23] but, while this shows that they saw sanctity in duty or in God's ordering of things, it hardly shows that they believed in the sanctity of *life* itself, of the union of body and soul that constitutes a human being. Moreover, if the Pythagoreans believed in the transmigration of souls and in the associated notion of the body *(soma)* as the tomb *(sema)* of the soul from which it seeks to escape, as Burnet and others hold they did,[24] then they can hardly have believed in the sanctity of bodily life as such, even though they regarded suicide as absolutely wrong. As for abortion, Edelstein says that the Pythagoreans had to proscribe it because they considered it a man's duty to beget children so as to leave behind him more worshipers of the gods,[25] which hardly suggests that they proscribed it out of a respect for life as such; but he also says that they had to regard abortion as murder because they maintained that one is a living being, uniting body and soul, from the moment of conception on, which would suggest that they did respect life as such, if they did not also hold to the *soma-sema* doctrine or appeal to the principle that one must not interfere with God's schedules of arrival and departure. The Pythagoreans believed in a qualified respect for life, apparently as an absolute principle, but probably regarded it as derivative from some more basic consideration and not as ultimate.

(4) In connection with Christianity, as well as with paganism, one may ask whether its opposition to abortion etc. entails its being committed to the sanctity of bodily life as such. It does, if one simply means by belief in the sanctity of life, belief that abortion etc. are wrong.[26] As we saw, however, whether or not one believes in the sanctity of bodily life as such depends on one's reasons for regarding it as wrong to shorten or prevent such life. We may, then, ask why Christianity regards this as wrong.

The usual answer is to say, as Lecky does, either that the human soul is immortal or that it is immortal and therefore has "inestimable value." But this reply will not do the job, because, as we just saw, one might hold that the body is a tomb from which the soul seeks to be free; from a soul's immortality or inestimable value it does not follow that it is wrong to prevent or break up a union of body and soul. Another answer is to say that man is to be respected because he was created in the image of God, but, again, it is not clear that this by itself means that we should respect each union of soul and body as wrong to interfere with, especially since God is immaterial. A third reply is to argue that after God had created man by shaping a body and infusing it with a soul, he looked at the result and "saw that it was good," indeed "very good."[27] Assuming that this was true and remained true after the Fall, I am once more not sure the wanted conclusion follows. For the judgment that the creation was good can hardly be a moral judgment and would seem to be an aesthetic or quasi-aesthetic one in the sense mentioned earlier; it would then not necessarily entail, without further ado, that it is morally wrong to kill any creature, plant, animal, or human, as the sequel in Genesis seems to show.

A better answer than these is to say that we are to respect human life because God does—because He loves His creatures, or because He commands us not to kill ourselves or others and to love our neighbors as we love ourselves. This line of thought is stressed by Paul Ramsey: "The value of a human life is ultimately grounded in the value God is placing on it. . . . [A human being's] dignity is 'an alien dignity,' an evaluation that is not of him but placed upon him by the divine decree [or by the act of divine love]."[28] As Ramsey notes, however, this approach does not ascribe intrinsic value to a human life; it makes the sanctity of such a life dependent on its relation to God, not on "something inherent in man." In this sense, it does not entail a belief in the sanctity of human life *as such*—that is, a belief that preventing or shortening a human union of body and soul is *as such* wrong either *ceteris paribus* or absolutely.

To this, of course, a Christian may reply, "So be it! All that matters is that preventing and shortening human lives are morally wrong; whether they are morally wrong *as such* or not is unimportant." This may be, but then at least we must be clear just what we are claiming if we claim that life has sanctity and on what ground. In any case, we may note that at least two Christians reject the belief that "physiological life" has sanctity, whether intrinsically or otherwise. Joseph Fletcher quotes with approval the following from William Temple: "The notion that life is absolutely sacred is Hindu or Buddhist, not Christian. . . . [The] belief that life, physiological life, is sacrosanct . . . is not a Christian idea at all; for, if it were, the martyrs would be wrong. If the sanctity is *in* life, it must be wrong to give your life for a noble cause as well as to take another's. But the Christian must be ready to give life gladly for his faith, as for a noble cause. Of course, this implies that, *as compared with some things*, the loss of life is a small evil; if so, then, *as compared with some other things*, the taking of life is a small injury."[29] If Temple and Fletcher are right, then the idea of the sanctity of life is not a Christian concept and we must look elsewhere for its source—perhaps in romanticism, evolutionism, or Oriental thought. However, Temple and Fletcher show at most that Christianity does not entail that it is always actually wrong to shorten a human life—or to give one up—and this is compatible with holding that it is always presumptively or prima facie wrong, or wrong other things being equal, to do so. It may then still be that Christianity does essentially assert the sanctity of human life at least in this sense, and I believe it does, but my question is, "Why? On what grounds?," and I have argued that some of the usual replies will not do, or at least will not serve to show that human life (bodily or physiological) has sanctity or should be respected *as such*.

Yet one more reply of this sort is to argue that it is wrong for anyone to end the bodily life of anyone else, or even of himself, because what happens to one in this life determines what future his soul will have in the hereafter. For example, it has been held, according to Lecky, that if one kills an animated fetus, one is dooming a soul to hell forever, since it will then perish without having been baptized.[30] Granted the premises, such reasoning does show that bodily life is of crucial importance and that ending it may be wrong, but it does not show that it is wrong as such, or even that it is wrong under all circumstances.

There is, however, another line of thought in Christianity. In rejecting the body-soul dualisms of the Pythagoreans, Platonists, and Gnostics, including the *soma-sema* conception of human life, Christian thinkers have often insisted on the unity and goodness of man's nature as a combination of body and soul, citing, among other things, the doctrines of the Incarnation and of the resurrection of the body as supporting such a view.[31] They use this line of thinking to show that the body is not inherently bad and to provide a basis for rejecting asceticism, not so much to establish the sanctity of the life of each soul in its body (that is, the wrongness of preventing or shortening it), but obviously it may be used to show this too. But it still leaves open the question of whether human bodily life has moral sanctity as such or only because of some relationship in which it stands to God.

(5) Some kind of belief in the sanctity of human life, though not necessarily in that of life in the body as such, is involved in the long tradition that evolved among Catholic philosophers and theologians out of Aquinas's discussion of self-defense—namely, the tradition that centers on a distinction between what one intends or directly wills and what one permits and only indirectly wills, together with the so-called doctrine of double effect. As I understand it, writers in this tradition at first applied this distinction and doctrine to self-defense, capital punishment, and war, as well as to other issues. They were in effect taking it as an absolute principle that it is always wrong intentionally to take a human life—whether it be as an end or as a means to some other end—the life of an assailant, criminal, or enemy soldier, as a means to saving one's own, protecting society, or defending one's country. All that is morally tolerable in this view is permitting people to die as an unintended (though foreseen) side effect of what one does in order to achieve some end other than their death. This position is hard to defend when the people in question are

attacking one's life or country, and not unquestionable even when they are guilty of murder. As a result, the tradition referred to has tended in more recent times to apply its distinction and doctrine only in conflict cases in which the life of an innocent human being is at stake. That is, it tends now to posit only the absolute sanctity of *innocent* and *noncombatant* human lives, and to apply the principle of double effect, not in cases of self-defense etc. but in cases involving abortion, euthanasia, suicide, self-sacrifice, judicial murder, sterilization, contraception, etc.

This shift involves moving to a somewhat limited, though still absolute and very significant, principle of respect for life—limited in two ways: first, in the way just indicated, by a kind of denial of the sanctity of the lives of certain criminals and combatants, or at least by a belief that they have in some way forfeited or exempted themselves from the right not to be killed as means to an end other than their death (for it is still regarded as absolutely wrong to take even their deaths as an *end*); and, second, in another way, by the assertion that while it is wrong or intolerable to take an innocent life *intendingly*, even as a means, it is not always wrong *voluntarily* to "let die," that is, to do something (perhaps an "act of omission") which has the result that innocent people die.

The core of this traditional Catholic position is the doctrine of double effect, the main thrust of which, for present purposes, is that it is always morally intolerable or wrong to take an innocent human life intentionally, either as an end or as a means to some other end, however good; but that it is sometimes morally permissible voluntarily to let a fetus or innocent person die —namely, when nothing evil is taken either as an end or as a means and when permitting the death is justified by "proportionate reasoning" of considerable weight. Applied to the crucial case already mentioned, this doctrine implies that it is wrong to kill the fetus in order to save both it and the mother, since to do so is to *intend* its death as a means to one's end, and that it is right to *permit* both to die even though one could save the mother. On the basis of this and other cases, as well as on other grounds, many recent Catholic writers are giving up or modifying the traditional position, especially the principle that it is absolutely wrong to bring about the death of a fetus or innocent person intentionally, no matter what the alternative may be.[32] Perhaps some of them are also giving up the belief in the sanctity of human life. But this does not follow; one can reject the tradition and still believe that it is always *prima facie* wrong either to kill an innocent person or to let one die voluntarily.

I said that the tradition in question believes in an absolute but limited kind of sanctity of human life. This does not mean that it believes, even in this limited way, in the sanctity of human bodily life *as such*. Whether it does or not depends on why it regards the taking of an innocent life as wrong, and it may answer this question in different ways—for example, by saying that it is wrong because it is against God's law. It need not say, and may or may not hold, that it is wrong just because it is the shortening of the bodily life of some human being.

(6) It is, therefore, clear that Pythagoreanism played a small part, and the Judeo-Christian tradition a large one, in the evolution of the view that Abortion etc. are morally wrong, but it is rather less clear that they generated the idea of the sanctity of human bodily or earthly life as such. *If* they did not, where might *this* idea (if it is around at all) have come from? Well, as was intimated, it may be a product of such more or less opposite movements as the Renaissance, romanticism (including Hegelian Idealism), and evolutionism. These movements certainly did bring about some new ways of speaking about life, or rather Life, the kind of talk about life that we sometimes find in Dewey and Whitehead—for example, the idea that life has no aim beyond itself, no end except more life, that education is life and life is the subject matter of education, and so on.[33] Commenting forcefully on this development of "vitalism" and its "eulogistic use of the word *life*," Morris Cohen wrote:

That the continuance of mere physical life is an absolute moral good seems to be axiomatic in current ethics. It serves as a basis for the unqualified moral condemnation of all forms of suicide and euthanasia . . . this setting up of mere life as an absolute moral good . . . is inconsistent with the moral approval of the hero or the martyr who throws away life for the sake of honor or conscience . . . we cannot . . . dispense with the classical problem of defining the good and discriminating it from the evil of life. . . . Instead of life we want the good life. . . . Conduct, science, and art . . . depend on rational discrimination. . . . The essence of the romantic use of the [term] *life* . . . is that it avoids this necessary task.[34]

Actually, Cohen is somewhat confusing the view that mere life is good and the view that it is absolutely wrong to end or give up a life. He also obscures the fact that those who adopt the evolutionary or romantic view of life are not typically against abortion, euthanasia, or population control. Still, he does put his finger on a kind of "worship of mere life" that does not stem from either classical antiquity or Christianity. It stems, in fact, at least partly from the evolutionism that arose in the nineteenth century, which did ascribe a kind of sanctity to life, human or nonhuman, by taking life as the end or good and conduct as right or wrong according as it promotes or opposes life—one's own or life in general. As Sidgwick puts it, "Life (without breadth) is the ultimate end which certain writers of the evolutionist school are disposed to lay down instead of Happiness."[35] One must, however, be careful in interpreting evolutionary writers. Herbert Spencer appears to do this sort of thing when he writes, ". . . the conduct to which we apply the name good, is the relatively more evolved conduct . . . evolution becomes the highest possible when the conduct simultaneously achieves the greatest totality of life in self, in offspring, and in fellow men . . . [and] the conduct called good rises to the conduct conceived as best when it fulfills all three classes of ends at the same time."[36] But, as Sidgwick points out, "Substantially Mr. Spencer gives the most decided preference to 'pleasure' over 'life' as ultimate end. Immediately after the passage before quoted, which seems to take conduciveness to 'totality of life' as the criterion of 'good' conduct, he says there is an assumption involved in this view—namely, that such conduct brings a 'surplus of agreeable feelings.' . . . He is therefore an Evolutionist Hedonist, not an Evolutionist pure."[37]

Discussing the pure "nonhedonistic" view that "Life (without breadth) is the ultimate end," Sidgwick argues, first, that "an ethical end cannot be proved by biology," second, that the fact that we must live in order to live well "does not make life identical with living well," third, that such prohibitions as that of killing or suicide are not self-evident but, so far as rational, rest ultimately on utilitarian grounds, and, fourth, that Spencer was right in "substantially" equating the good with pleasure rather than with life, since life may be painful and so is not desirable as such, but only when it is pleasant: "I quite admit that . . . part of the function of morality consists in maintaining such habits and sentiments as are necessary to the continued existence, in full numbers, of a society of human beings. . . . But this is not because the mere existence of human organisms, even if prolonged to eternity, appears to me in any way desirable; it is only assumed to be so because it is supposed to be accompanied by Consciousness on the whole desirable; it is therefore this Desirable Consciousness which we must regard as ultimate Good."[38]

However this may be, it should be emphasized that even when those who hold this evolutionary view have taken life to be the ultimate end, they have not typically drawn the conclusion that abortion etc. are morally wrong. The view has therefore not tended to support the "pro-life" movement that has recently been lobbying for this conclusion, even though it has generated a kind of regard for Life.

(7) While Sidgwick was attacking naturalistic ethics of a vitalistic kind, he did so without any reference to Judeo-Christian doctrines or to religion or supernaturalism of any kind. Indeed, his discussion signalizes the fact that, at least in British moral philosophy, questions relating to the sanctity of life (while not

raised in those words) had long been debated in very different terms. Roughly, the issue as he and his colleagues saw it was this: are any principles pertaining to the prevention or shortening of human bodily life self-evident or deducible from others that are self-evident, or are such matters to be determined entirely by considerations of utility, by considerations relating to one's own good or happiness or to that of the world? That is, the basic debate, as Sidgwick's review of the "methods of ethics" shows, was between deontological intuitionism, and teleologism, egoistic or utilitarian (i.e., universalistic). This was the secular and philosophical form that the discussion took for those who held ethics to have a "bottom"—independent of revelation or of the special doctrines of the Judeo-Christian religions—many of whom were divines and counted themselves as Christian: the Clarkes, Samuel and John, Berkeley, Butler, Price, and Paley, for example. Some believed in the sanctity of life in the sense of believing that certain sorts of treatment of life are self-evidently or demonstrably wrong as such, if not absolutely, then at least when other things are equal; the others (including Sidgwick) denied it in the sense of holding that such treatment is right or wrong depending on whether or not it is to one's good or to that of the world. Outside of theology, among moral philosophers, though with less reliance on intuition and self-evidence, this is essentially the form in which the debate goes on today. It may even be, then, that the idea of the moral sanctity of human life really appeared not with Christianity but with the modern moral philosophers, so much influenced by the Stoics, who held "these truths to be self-evident." At any rate, this idea is nicely exemplified by Samuel Clarke when he writes, "it is without dispute more fit and reasonable in itself that I should preserve the life of an innocent man . . . or deliver him from any imminent danger, though I have never made any promise so to do, than that I should suffer him to perish, or take away his life, without any reason or provocation at all."[39] This does not say that suffering an innocent person to perish, or even taking his life, is always absolutely wrong, nor does it say that innocent life has sanctity simply as life, but it does proclaim the prima facie wrongness of taking an innocent person's life or of letting him die, and proclaims it as self-evident without any religious premises.

(8) Here I should mention Kant, who, though not an intuition-ist, was a deontologist and did proscribe murder and suicide on a priori and nonreligious grounds. His arguments in his later works are well known. Earlier, in his *Lectures on Ethics*, he said as a preface to his discussion of suicide:

In fact, however, our life is entirely conditioned by our body, so that we cannot conceive of a life not mediated by the body and we cannot make use of our freedom except through the body. It is, therefore, obvious that the body constitutes a part of ourselves. If a man destroys his body, and so his life, he does it by the use of his will, which is itself destroyed in the process. But to use the power of a free will for its own destruction is self-contradictory. If freedom is the condition of life it cannot be employed to abolish life and so to destroy and abolish itself. To use life for its own destruction, to use life for producing lifelessness, is self-contradictory.[40]

Though against suicide, Kant did not regard preservation of one's life as one's highest duty; it may, he thought, be morally necessary to sacrifice one's life to avoid violating another duty, but doing this is not suicide. Thus he accorded bodily life a kind of sanctity independent of any divine command and of any immortality the soul may have. It is also clear, however, that what bothered him was not the thought that in suicide one is using one's bodily life as a means to its own destruction, but the fact that bodily life is a necessary condition of our "life" in the sense of the use of our will or freedom, and that therefore, in committing suicide, one is using one's will or freedom as a means to *its* own destruction. Bodily life for Kant (here) has sanctity, but only indirectly, because it is necessary for the life of the will.

Of course, one may argue that, historically and causally or genetically, the Christian religion was necessary as a precondition of such views as Clarke's and Kant's, and this may be true. It still may be true, however, that those views are *logically* independent of any religious beliefs—as Clarke and Kant thought they were.

(9) But whether fairness is a duty independently of utility or not, we must be fair (even) to the utlilitarians and point out that while they deny that abortion etc. are wrong simply as such, even they do or can subscribe to the sanctity of human life in at least two ways. (a) In a way, they are inheritors of the Christian ethics of love (as the deontologists are inheritors of the ethics of the Ten Commandments). They insist that each and every person affected—or even each and every sentient being—is to be considered when we are trying to determine what is right and what is wrong; to this extent at least they may and do regard it as prima facie wrong to harm any such being or to take its life when no *greater* good is to be gained by doing so. (b) Although an act utilitarian can regard rules prohibiting abortion etc. only as rules of thumb arising out of previous calculations, a rule utilitarian may regard rules relating to the sanctity of life in a stronger light. As the example of Berkeley shows, he may even believe in absolute, exceptionless rules.[41] That is, he may argue that, for the general welfare, it is necessary that we all accept and conform to certain prohibitions taken to have no exceptions, and, further, that among those prohibitions are those that forbid the preventing or shortening of human life. Such a line of argument, whatever its plausibility, would, if successful, establish the sanctity of human life—in the sense of establishing the principles that abortion, suicide, killing, etc. are wrong—on a utilitarian basis. It would, of course, not show that preventing or shortening human lives is always wrong (even prima facie) *as such*, but it would yield the same practical conclusions.

(10) It may be asked whether anyone has actually denied that human life has moral sanctity, directly or indirectly, at least in some qualified and prima facie sense. The answer is that some social-contract theorists have denied or would deny this—namely, those who hold that we have no moral duties toward those who

do not or cannot (e.g., animals) enter into the relevant social contract with us, or that such persons and beings have no moral rights in relation to us.[42]

5.

My discussion of the idea of respect for human life, except for some opening distinctions, has thus far been historical. Now I should like to say something systematic, by way of indicating some of my own views. The main question is: What, if anything, makes it wrong, at least presumptively, to prevent or shorten a human life? There are a number of possible lines of reply, some religious, resting on specifically religious premises, and some not. We cannot answer that what makes it wrong is the fact, if it is a fact, that human life has sanctity (or dignity, intrinsic worth, etc.), since this is a tautology. However, we can say, first of all, that what makes shortening or preventing human bodily life wrong is simply the fact that it is bodily life of a certain sort, that human bodily life has sanctity as such or in itself; and, in saying this, we may hold that this is so either because bodily or physical life has sanctity as such or because human physical life has. If one holds the former, one is holding that "x is (or will be) living" entails "It is wrong, at least prima facie, to end or prevent its life," or, in other words, that plant and animal life also has sanctity —thus raising the question of comprehensive respect for life, which we will come to. If one holds the latter, one is believing that it is wrong to check, end, or prevent human bodily life, not just because it is bodily life but because it is human. Then we may ask what it adds to say that it is human, and I assume that the reply cannot be merely that it takes the form of a featherless biped or laughs. The reply must mention some essential, inherent, or intrinsic feature of human beings other than mere physical life. This could be the fact that they are conscious, have feelings, etc., and then it would imply that some nonhuman animal life has sanctity and should be respected too; or it could be the fact that human beings have reason, purposes, ambitions, hopes, and ideals, or that their souls are immortal. Just what one would mention here depends on what characteristics one regards as inherent in man, and this varies from view to view, especially from naturalistic to supernaturalistic ones. The point, however, is that, if one takes this present line, then one is saying that what gives human life sanctity is not the fact that it is life but the fact that it is human—i.e., the fact that it is accompanied by rationality, moral capacity, immortality, or whatever is supposed to be distinctive of human beings. And then one is not believing in the sanctity of physical life as such, but in the sanctity of rationality, morality, immortality, or whatever. One may still believe that it is wrong, at least prima facie, to prevent or shorten a human life, but *only* if one *also* holds that doing so interferes with, puts an end to, or otherwise adversely affects someone's rationality, moral capacity, immortality, or whatever, not just because it affects someone's *life*. One would, then, be hard put to show that it would be wrong, even prima facie, to end the life of a human being who has become completely and incurably comatose.

Perhaps I should remark here that I do not see how merely being immortal would confer sanctity on human life. Would a redwood tree *(Sequoia sempervirens)* have sanctity if (or only if) it were to live forever if not cut down? More important, however, is a further point: if one believes that the human soul is immortal, and hence that *its* (spiritual) life cannot be ended by killing the body it may be in, then it becomes harder, not easier, to prove that it is wrong to kill that body. For then one must show that killing that body will adversely affect the soul's destiny in the hereafter or that it countervenes a divine ordinance, and these are things it is not easy to show, things which it may be necessary to take on faith, and which may therefore reasonably be doubted.

A second kind of answer to the question of why it is wrong to end or prevent a human life is to say that what makes it wrong is not any feature inherent to such life but some extrinsic or relational fact about it—for example, that it contributes to the perfection of the universe or to the glory of God, or that it stands in some other relation to God, such as that of being loved by Him. On such views it will be wrong, perhaps absolutely wrong, to prevent or shorten a human life, not because this is in any way wrong as such, but only because it entails interfering with the perfection of the universe, with something God loves, and so on. If human life did (does) not stand in such relations, there would be (is) nothing wrong in blocking or ending it.

A third possiblity is that one might argue that what makes it morally wrong to block or end human life is the fact that it is intrinsically good in a nonmoral sense or sacred in the special sense mentioned earlier. I myself doubt, however, that human life is always or necessarily good in itself (unless this means only that it is prima facie wrong to interfere with it), and also that its being good in itself is a necessary condition of its being wrong to block it or end it. As for its being sacred, if this means something different from its being wrong to block or end it, then I become doubtful that this is either a necessary or a sufficient condition of its being *morally* wrong to prevent or shorten a bodily life. In any case, we still have the further question of what makes such a life good or sacred, and then the answer must take either our first or second lines, and has, in effect, been discussed.

Views claiming that some religious premise is a necessary or sufficient condition of a belief in the moral sanctity of human bodily life I shall not further discuss. Such premises may be necessary or sufficient for a belief in the *sacredness* of human life, but I am not convinced that they are even relevant to a belief that it is *morally* wrong to interfere with such life. Now let us look at what I called *unqualified* belief in the moral sanctity of human life—that is, the claim that every kind of preventing or shortening of bodily human life is wrong, either absolutely or prima facie (if intentional). I said I doubted that anyone has ever really held this, and now I want to add that it seems incredible. For it entails that it is at least prima facie wrong to block intentionally the starting or the fruition, not only of a nascent, but even of any possible human life. Strictly, it means that it is prima facie or absolutely wrong to refrain from sexual intercourse (or artificial insemination) whenever the opportunity presents itself, if the woman is capable of impregnation and the resulting child will be viable as a human. In fact, refraining will be actually wrong, if one hasn't anything else or better to do. Surely, "Be fruitful, and multiply, and replenish the earth" never meant this! Even if one regards contraception and early abortion as wrong, what about rhythm, voluntary celibacy, or plain disinclination?

One might, of course, insist that it is always prima facie wrong not to start a possible human being on its way, but add that its wrongness is very easily outweighed by other considerations, maybe even by the fact that one would rather do something else. But then the idea of the sanctity of human life has very little, if any, substance left. In any case, however, it seems clear that an unqualified belief in the sanctity of human physical life as an *absolute* principle, always wrong to violate, *is* incredible. Let us then consider the more qualified belief that acts of ending such a life are morally wrong, prima facie or absolutely.

While I am not sure that or when a fetus is a human being or a person, I myself find it hard to deny that, since it is a nascent human being and person, it is prima facie wrong intentionally to destroy it or let it die.[43] I doubt, however, that this is true simply because the fetus is alive. But it seems clear to me that it is, at most, only prima facie and not absolutely wrong, though I do not believe that its prima facie wrongness is as easily outweighed or overridden as many recent defenders of abortion do. More generally, when I take the moral point of view, it seems to me clear that some kind of qualified respect for bodily human life is indeed called for, though not just because it is life. It is called for because human life normally is or can be so much more than just life, in ways in which floral and other faunal life is not and cannot be. That is, it is called for by the fact that, for human beings as we know them in our ordinary experience, bodily life is a necessary condition of their being conscious, joyful, happy, moral, religious, or fulfilled. This means, as I see it, that bodily life, even in the case of a human being, does not have sanctity *as such*, but only qua being a seat for the realization of something more. In this sense, respect for human life—for what I called quantity of bodily life—turns out to be based on concern about the quality of such life after all. It also follows, of course, that our respect for human bodily life is or should be indirect and derivative, rather than direct or basic. To this extent Morris Cohen was right. I do think, however, that the moral sanctity of human life is at least partly intrinsic, not because it is intrinsic to life but because it is based on some inherent feature of human beings; that is, I do not think it is based entirely on something extrinsic to them or relational, as Ramsey seems to think.

It does not follow from this view that abortion is not prima facie wrong, or that fetal life has no sanctity, for a fetus is, as such, on its way to being human. Nor does it follow that abortion is never right; it does seem to me, for instance, that it is not wrong to perform an abortion when the only alternative is to let both the mother and the fetus die. It also does not follow, of course, that animal life has no sanctity, since at least some animals are capable of something more than just being alive. It does, however, follow that it is not necessarily wrong morally, perhaps not even prima facie wrong, to end or let end the life of a person who has become hopelessly comatose, at least if it is done under certain conditions.

6.

Let us now take up respect for life in general—plant and animal as well as human—still meaning by "life" bodily or organic life. Earlier I called this *comprehensive* respect for life, the belief in the sanctity of all organic life on earth and elsewhere. One can believe in the sanctity of human life without believing in that of all kinds of life; indeed, historically, human life has long and usually been accorded a sanctity not accorded to plant or animal life. However, if one holds that all life has sanctity, absolute or *ceteris paribus*, one must hold that human life has it too. In fact, we saw that, on one view, human life has sanctity because and only because it is a form of life, and that, if one maintains this, then one is committed to comprehensive respect for life (or at least for animal life). We should also notice that respect for life can assume any and all of the forms taken by respect for human life: it can be religious or moral, qualified or unqualified, and so on. I shall assume that this is clear, and will not run through the various possibilities.

In the way of history I shall be brief. In the East, as Temple noticed, comprehensive respect for life was advocated long ago in Hinduism and Jainism, but in the West it is, I believe, a relatively latecomer. Remember that love of nature, admiration of nature, and curiosity about nature need not involve any moral respect for nature or life in my sense, for it may be sentimental or, if not, purely aesthetic, quasi-aesthetic, or cognitive. At any rate, the Genesis view that God gave man "dominion over the fish of the sea, and over the fowl of the air, and over every living thing that moveth upon the earth" seems to have been dominant in the Judeo-Christian tradition, though it went together with a kind of respect for all of creation as the handiwork of God and as something he saw to be "very good." Even so, one finds in that tradition some feeling that living things are not to be destroyed or even prevented from coming into being wantonly, for no reason at all, or only for pleasure. It seems only that it is not insisted that the reasons need to be very good; the Jains at any rate took a much more absolute view, insisting that the reasons are never good enough. Later, as Cohen points out, there was a kind of praise of life in some of the romantics, which he exemplifies by William James's remark about the then new philosophy: "It lacks logical rigor, but it has the tang of life."[44] As we saw, there was, also in the nineteenth century, a kind of evolutionary ethics that took the promotion of life as the end by which right and wrong are to be determined: we are to do what most advances life in length and/or in breadth, in the individual, in the species, and/or in the world. In short, we are to act in accordance with the movement of the *élan vital.* There were also related "vitalistic" ethics or ethics of the "affirmation of life" of various sorts—in Fouillée, Guyau, Nietzsche, Eucken, and maybe Bergson. I have suggested that these developments may have had a hand in the development of the idea of the sanctity of life that is our topic, but I should again point out that they hardly tend to support any conclusion to the effect that Abortion etc. are all wrong, though they may be responsible for a eulogistic use of the word "life."

This is where I must bring in Albert Schweitzer's view, including his picture of the history of ethics.[45] It is well known that he advocated an ethic of "reverence for life," not just human life but *all* life. He saw such an ethic as the culmination of a long debate involving three previous types of ethic:

1. the ethics of rational pleasure, which he describes as "egoistic utilitarian" and attributes to some ancients and some moderns
2. the modern "social-utilitarian" ethics of altruism or self-devotion, at least partly due to Christianity
3. the ethics of "self-perfecting," active and/or passive, under which he places the various ethical theories of Plato, Aristotle, the Stoics, the Jewish prophets, the antiegoistic and antiutilitarian British moralists, Spinoza, Kant, Fichte, Schopenhauer, Nietzsche, the Hegelian idealists—and the Indians and "the great moralists of China."

All of these, he maintains, are inadequate in one way or another. The first cannot account for self-sacrifice, and he drops it from further consideration. The second and third each leave out and cannot generate what the other takes as central. But they may be combined in a certain way, involving their becoming "cosmic" and "mystical" and yielding (somehow) his culminating fourth ethic, that of reverence for life, of "responsibility without limit toward all that lives." With this we finally come—at least in the West—to the full conception and ethics of the sanctity of *all* life, of comprehensive, unqualified, and, I think, direct respect for life. "A man is truly ethical only when he obeys the compulsion to help all life which he is able to assist, and shrinks from injuring anything that lives. He does not ask how far this or that life deserves one's sympathy as being valuable, nor . . . whether and to what degree it is capable of feeling. Life as such is sacred to him. He tears no leaf from a tree, plucks no flower, and takes care to crush no insect."[46]

More recently, as has been intimated, some such comprehensive ethic of respect for life (and/or nature) seems to be behind some of the thinking going on, not only in bioethics but also in what I called ecoethics.[47] In such views, most of our historical moralities and systems of ethics have been grievously anthropocentric, as Schweitzer charged. Such views are, I believe, rarely religious in a traditional Western theistic sense; sometimes they are oriental in spirit, sometimes they are aesthetic or quasi-aesthetic in motivation, sometimes they are animistic in their conception of nature, and sometimes they stress the continuity of man, evolutionary and nonevolutionary, with the rest of nature. Jonas, one of the more interesting writers I have read in preparing this paper, is tempted by them in the course of his "reflections on the new tasks of ethics," and seems to be trying to find some support for them in the Jewish religion.

In the light of these historical remarks, together with those made earlier, it looks to me as if the idea of respect for life that underlies the "pro-life" movements in recent bio- and ecoethical discussions is really a loosely related family of ethical beliefs resulting from a confluence of a variety of sources: the Judeo-Christian religion, deontological moral philosophy, romanticism, evolutionism, and certain Oriental systems of thought. In particular, it looks as if three rather different kinds of respect for life are involved in those pro-life movements: a noncomprehensive one consisting of a belief that abortion etc. are wrong, absolutely or presumptively; a comprehensive one that eulogizes Life but does not entail any such opposition to abortion etc.; and another comprehensive one, of which Schweitzer is an example, that both reverences life and believes that abortion etc. are wrong.

In the way of systematic discussion of this comprehensive respect for life, I must be even briefer. Leaving aside the question of respect for *nature*, let us confine ourselves to that of respect for *life*, floral and faunal. Then I stand ready to allow that some ways of treating animals that are capable of feeling fear and pain are prima facie morally wrong, and that there is something wrong with killing such animals for the fun of it. But I am not sure that it is wrong to prevent their coming into life or to shorten their lives when they do, at least if this is done without causing fear or pain and is of some good to us. I certainly do not see that we have any moral duties to animals that are not conscious of fear, pain, or pleasure, or to plants (even if talking to plants does help them to flourish!). Unlike Brennan, I have not come to recognize the "postulate," ethical or not, "that every living thing has a prima facie claim on life and that if we override that claim in a particular instance we should be able to justify our action by sound reasons."[48] In short, I see no sanctity in mere life, in life that is not at least capable of conscious aversion, desire, enjoyment, fear, relief, pain, satisfaction, or suffering—and rather little in life that is capable of these but incapable of thought, purpose, hope, regret, and the like. I am all for ecology, environmental quality, conservation, bird watching, and game refuges, but not because I think biological life has any moral sanctity as such, but only because birds and many other animals are capable of feeling and suffering, and because they and the rest of nature are aesthetically, cognitively, instrumentally, and perhaps even emotionally and socially, valuable to beings like us.[49] Such considerations suffice to show that certain ways of "relating" to nonhuman nature are morally wrong, as ecoethical moralists wish to claim.

The most plausible basis for a comprehensive respect for life similar to Schweitzer's, to my mind, would be an animistic metaphysics of the Leibniz-Whitehead type, but, while I am not entirely unsympathetic with the idea of such a metaphysics, I am very dubious about the project of ascribing intrinsic value to lives or spirits that have no conscious experience whatsoever, and hence also about saying that we ought or ought not (morally) to treat them in certain ways, let alone saying that they ought or ought not (morally) to treat each other (and us?) in certain ways. Much depends here on the amount of analogy with ourselves that one is willing to ascribe to such lives or spirits, and on the extent to which one is willing to stretch the categories of value and morality.

7.

I have now made a good many distinctions and perhaps some points, historical, analytical, or normative. Some of the main nonhistorical points may be summarized as follows:

1. The sanctity of human life (bodily) is not relevant to the discussion of all bio- and ecoethical questions, but only to those involving the preventing or shortening of human life. Others involve the sanctity of individuality or personality, or quality rather than quantity of life. The sanctity of bodily human life should be distinguished from that of individuality or personality, even if there is a connection.
2. Mere life, whether that of a vegetable, animal, or human organism, has no moral sanctity as such, though it may have aesthetic and other kinds of nonmoral value, and may be a necessary condition of consciousness, rationality, or morality.
3. Life has moral sanctity, but only where it is a condition of something more, as it is in humans, fetuses, and some animals.
4. This something must be something inherent—consciousness, feeling, reason—in such living beings, but not just being immortal, not something wholly extrinsic.
5. Even then the moral sanctity of human life (bodily) is not absolute, it is considerable, at least from the moral point of view, but it is only prima facie or presumptive.
6. The only tenable view, then, is a derivative, qualified, and noncomprehensive ethics of respect for life.

I have not tried to prove these points but only to state them in such a way as to make them clear and convincing, and to provide a kind of history of the ideas involved in them. Three other remarks are necessary in conclusion. First, on the view just formulated, the principle of respect for life is not basic but derivative; it is, however, not just a maxim or rule of thumb such as an act utilitarian or situational moralist might take it to be. In any case, in order to solve any of the actual problems of medical or environmental ethics—for example, abortion or population control—one must do more than merely appeal to that principle. One must appeal to the full body of all relevant basic ethical principles, old or new, of which that of the sanctity of life is a corollary, and one must make use of all the available factual knowledge bearing on the problem. Second, I have talked as if saying that life has sanctity means only that it is wrong to treat it in certain ways. This can, of course, be expressed more positively by saying that it is right or obligatory not to treat it in those ways, or that people, fetuses, etc. have a *right* to life, though one must use the right-to-life way of speaking with some care if one uses it at all. Can one put it yet more positively by saying that it is right or obligatory to treat life in the opposite ways, by lengthening or multiplying it? In some *very* qualified sense I think the answer is yes, but I leave this question open here. A yes answer would add another dimension to my ethics of respect for life, but it would not otherwise affect what I have said. Secondly, I have mentioned law, but have confined my discussion to moral questions. As Glanville Williams's title, *The Sanctity of Life and the Criminal Law*, indicates, however, our subject comes up in the law also. Indeed, any system of law almost necessarily embodies and enforces at least a qualified respect for human life—for example, in proscribing certain forms of killing. It is then a very live question whether our law should permit abortion, euthanasia, suicide, the hunting of animals, or the trampling of plants. I assume that it must permit the eating of at least some plants and seeds, but for the rest I leave such questions open too.

NOTES

1. *In Memoriam*, LV.

2. Cf. Hans Jonas, *Philosophical Essays* (Englewood Cliffs, N.J.: Prentice-Hall Inc., 1974), pp. 12, 17, 107, 163. For a good corrective argument see J. G.

THE ETHICS OF RESPECT FOR LIFE 61

Milhaven, *Toward a New Catholic Morality* (Garden City, N.Y.: Image Books, 1972), p. 225.

3. "The Sanctity of Life," in D. L. Labby (ed.), *Life or Death* (Seattle: University of Washington Press, 1968), pp. 29 ff, 32, 8-10.

4. See, e.g., Jonas, *op. cit.,* p. 163.

5. See Herbert Spencer, *The Data of Ethics* (New York: A. L. Burt Co., n.d.), chap. 2, para. 9.

6. Cf. R. S. Downie and E. Telfer, *Respect for Persons* (London: Allen and Unwin, 1969), p. 18.

7. See my "On Saying the Ethical Thing," *Proceedings and Addresses of the American Philosophical Association* 39 (1966): 21-42.

8. See his *Analysis of Knowledge and Valuation* (La Salle, Ill.: Open Court, 1946), p. 390

9. Cf., e.g., Jonas, *op. cit.,* pp. 17, 107, 180; Labby, *op. cit.,* pp. xviii, 58, 71.

10. Cf. Jonas *op. cit.,* p. 107.

11. M. J. Savage, *The Morals of Evolution* (Boston: G. H. Ellis, 1880), p. 22.

12. *Saul*, IX.

13. Cf. Ramsey, "The Morality of Abortion," in Labby, *op. cit.,* pp. 74 ff; Jonas, *op. cit.,* pp. 179 ff.

14. Jonas, *op. cit.,* pp. 9, 12 ff, 18 ff, 38.

15. Cf. Ramsey, *op. cit.,* pp. 70 ff; Jonas, *op. cit.,* pp. 19 ff, 179 ff.

16. I shall continue to use the expression "sanctity of life," but only in the moral sense just indicated.

17. Cf. W. D. Ross, *The Right and the Good* (Oxford: Clarendon Press, 1930), pp. 19 ff.

18. W. E. H. Lecky, *History of European Morals from Augustus to Charlemagne,* 11th ed. (London: Longmans Green Co., 1894), II, 18, 20, 34. Also cf. H. Sidgwick, *Outlines of the History of Ethics* (London; Macmillan Co., 1931), pp. 122 ff.

19. Cf. Jonas, *op. cit.,* pp. 10, 179 ff; also Schweitzer and Brennan as cited below.

20. *The Sources of Western Morality* (New York: Charles Scribner's Sons, 1954), p. 24.

21. Cf. Lecky, *op. cit.,* II, 17-61, and Edelstein as cited next. Here and in what follows I use "abortion etc." as short for "abortion, euthanasia, contraception, suicide, etc."

22. For my references to Edelstein, see *Ancient Medicine: Selected Papers of Ludwig Edelstein,* ed. Owsei Temkin and C. Lilian Temkin (Baltimore: The Johns Hopkins Press, 1967), pp. 6, 14 ff, and *passim.*

23. Lecky, *op. cit.,* p. 43; Edelstein, *op. cit.,* p. 17.

24. Cf., e. g., J. Burnet, *Early Greek Philosophy,* 3d ed. (London: A. C. Black, 1920), pp. 277 ff, but also 295.

25. Edelstein, *Op. cit.,* pp. 18 ff.

26. As R. C. Mortimer does, *Christian Ethics* (London: Hutchinsons' University Library, 1950), chap. 8.

27. *Genesis* I.

28. Ramsey, *op. cit.,* pp. 72-74.

29. J. F. Fletcher, *Morals and Medicine* (Princeton, N.J.: Princeton University Press, 1954), p. 193.

30. Lecky, *op. cit.,* p. 23.

31. Cf., e.g., G. F. Thomas, *Christian Ethics and Moral Philosophy* (New York: Scribners, 1955), p. 159.

32. See R. A. McCormick, *Ambiguity in Moral Choice,* Pere Marquette Lecture, 1973; and Milhaven, *op. cit.,* pp. 128 ff, 225 ff.

33. For an example of such talk see Jonas, *op. cit.,* p. 13. I should also call attention to interesting historical remarks about "the modern life philosophy" by Hannah Arendt, *The Human Condition* (Garden City, N.Y.: Doubleday Anchor Books, 1959), pp. 285 ff, 375 ff, *passim.*

34. M. R. Cohen, *Reason and Nature* (New York: Harcourt Brace & Co., 1931), pp. 451, 457.

35. H. Sidgwick, *The Ethics of T. H. Green, H. Spencer, and J. Martineau* (London: Macmillan, 1902), p. 144.

36. Spencer, *op. cit.,* p. 27 ff. Cf. pp. 51, 61, 70, 81.

37. Sidgwick, *Ethics of T. H. Green,* pp. 145 ff.

38. Ibid. p. 144; *The Methods of Ethics,* 7th ed. (London: Macmillan, 1930), pp. xxxii, 355 ff, 396 ff.

39. Cf. D. D. Raphael, ed., *British Moralists, 1650-1800* (Oxford: Clarendon Press, 1969), I, 194.

40. Immanuel Kant, *Lectures on Ethics* (New York: Century Co., c. 1930), pp. 147 ff.

41. George Berkeley, *Passive Obedience,* 1712.

42. This position was probably taken by Hobbes and, possibly, by Rousseau.

43. Cf. M. A. Warren, "On the Moral and Legal Status of Abortion," *Monist* 57 (1973): 59. This position is also hard to defend, however; see M. Tooley, "Abortion and Infanticide," and J. J. Thomson, "A Defense of Abortion" in *The Rights and Wrongs of Abortion,* ed. M. Cohen, T. Nagel, and T. Scanlon (Princeton, N.J.: Princeton University Press, 1974).

44. Cohen, *op. cit.,* p. 450.

45. See *Civilization and Ethics,* 3d ed. (London: A. C. Black, 1949), chaps. 19-22.

46. Ibid., p. 243.

47. Cf. Jonas, *op. cit.,* chaps. 1, 8; J. G. Brennan, *Ethics and Morals* (New York: Harper & Row, 1973), pp. 337-44; Holmes Rolston III, "Is There an Ecological Ethic?," *Ethics* 85 (1975): 93-109.

48. Brennan, *op. cit.,* p. 344.

49. I am left unconvinced, even by Rolston's eloquent and perceptive argument in the essay cited in n. 47.

THREE

Sanford H. Kadish

RESPECT FOR LIFE AND REGARD FOR RIGHTS IN THE CRIMINAL LAW

Life is a unique kind of good because it is the necessary condition for the enjoyment of all other goods. Therefore every person by and large tends to value his life pre-eminently, and any society must place a high value on preserving it. As H. L. A. Hart has observed, "our concern is with social arrangements for continued existence, not with those of a suicide club."[1] But while the aim of survival affords "a reason why . . . law and morals should include a specific content,"[2] it obviously does not afford a reason why that content should include placing the survival of every person above all else. For while we value our own lives preeminently, it does not follow that we equally value other people's lives; their lives may conflict with rights we claim or with goods we value, including our own lives. Hence any society must face the problem of deciding when the life of some should yield to the claims or interests of others.

On the one hand, our society, like all others, has, over the centuries, produced a substantial consensus as to how these issues should be resolved. On the other hand, that consensus tends continually to be shaken by new events and new challenges. So in

1. Notes may be found on pp. 95–101.

recent years we have been divided and perplexed by such problems as bombing civilians in war, mass starvation elsewhere in the world, abortion, euthanasia, human medical experimentation, obtaining organs for transplant, and deciding who should be kept alive for how long by life-sustaining devices.

Having stated these issues, however, I shall not mention them again until the end because my principal subject will be the received consensus itself rather than the current uncertainties about its application. I shall dwell rather on those relatively settled judgments and understandings concerning the taking of human life that we seem to have arrived at. My purpose in doing this is to try to get at what lies beneath those judgments and understandings. I undertake this inquiry for its own sake—it will not solve the hard questions I referred to. Still, insofar as it exposes what we agree on and why, it may, as a by-product, contribute something to the debate on the issues of the day that trouble us.

Where, then, shall we look for those settled understandings? I propose we look to the criminal law insofar as it deals with actions that result or tend to result in loss of life. For in its provisions that direct when life should be taken, when it may be taken justifiably, and when taking it is prohibited and when permitted, we have a body of formulations that have evolved over time through reflective and tested examinations of what we regard as of greater or lesser value and of what we regard as right and wrong. We have, in short, some kind of map of our sentiments with respect to life to serve as a basis for securing our bearings on where we have come to stand.

Before proceeding to draw that map let me acknowledge that it cannot be a precise indication of our settled sentiments, partly because some problems of justified killing are, as we shall see, not clearly settled in the criminal law. Insofar as we shall have to speculate on what the law would be, we will be compromising with our model of drawing inferences from the settled consensus. Another reason that our map cannot be precise is that there are considerations other than our attitudes toward the wrongness and undesirability of actions that affect how we shape the criminal law. Some conduct that tends to result in loss of life might be judged strongly undesirable and yet be unprohibited by law either because it cannot be prevented by criminal threat, or, if it can, then in too small a degree in light of the undesirable consequences the attempt at prevention would entail. For similar reasons, some conduct that tends to preserve lives might be judged strongly desirable and yet be uncompelled by the criminal law. We will have to be careful, therefore, in drawing conclusions too hastily from what the criminal law does or does not prohibit, compel, or tolerate.

It will be helpful to state at the outset one such instance of a need for caution. I refer to excused actions—those that are relieved of criminal liability out of regard not to a judgment of the nature and quality of the actions (which would make them justified, rather than excused) but to the condition of the actor in the circumstances. So we should say of an excused action not that the actor was right to do as he did but that for one reason or another more could not fairly be demanded of him, at least by the criminal law.[3] Although it may not always be clear whether some particular defense (even self-defense, for example) operates as an excuse or a justification, to the extent that it is an excuse it does not represent the kind of judgment that serves our purposes. The same is true, of course, of homicidal actions that are partially excused, in the sense that a lesser punishment is indicated, for here too the judgment turns on the situation of the actor rather than on the rightness of the action.

MAPPING THE RULES OF THE CRIMINAL LAW

In presenting the rules of the criminal law, I will start with actions intended or known to kill.[4] These are actions that are generally prohibited by the criminal law of our own and every legal system, and typically with the severest penalties. The victim's consent to an intended killing is not a defense. Taking one's own life was a felony at the common law. Today it is no longer a crime, although attempted suicide is sometimes criminal and aiding another to commit suicide virtually always is criminal.

To these primary prohibitions, however, there are exceptions that have a special interest for us because they rest on a judgment that intentional killings in certain circumstances are right actions. These exceptional circumstances include cases in which the person killed is not a wrongdoer as well as those in which he is. The latter are more familiar and I will start with them.

Capital punishment has been defended even by natural-rights philosophers, like Kant and Locke, and has historically been the typical penal response to the most feared or serious crimes. While its moral legitimacy has been challenged,[5] it is on the whole an accepted part of our jurisprudence.[6]

Law-enforcement officials may kill in other circumstances as well. At common law, they may kill where reasonably believed necessary to prevent "violent" felonies, even those against property, and to apprehend any felon. Under some modern statutes, reflecting an enhanced regard for the life of the felon, they are limited to killing to prevent crimes that threaten death or serious bodily injury or to prevent the escape of a suspect who is armed or otherwise poses a threat to life if left at large.[7]

Private persons may justifiably take life largely in the same circumstances in which law-enforcement officials may, though, unlike such officials, they are never duty-bound to do so. A person is also privileged to kill in an overlapping but more specifically defined class of cases: he may kill an unlawful aggressor where it reasonably appears necessary to avoid either the imminent loss of his life or the imminent infliction of serious bodily injury upon him (which need not necessarily threaten his life, as in the case of kidnapping and forced sexual intercourse). A person may use force to defend his property, but, except to the extent that the threat to his property also constitutes a "violent felony," he may not go so far as to kill. To this exception, however, there are further exceptions. At common law one could kill to prevent being unlawfully dispossessed from one's home or indeed to prevent any threat to property occurring through a forcible entry of his dwelling. The latter exception survives in modern statutes as well.

There is division on whether an obligation to run away, when one knows he can safely do so, qualifies the right to kill in defense of one's person. The common law permitted a person to hold his ground, as do most states today. Those that require retreat, however, do not require that one run from his home or place of business.

Killing by a private person in defense of another is today generally allowed in the same circumstances as killing in defense of self. The common law and a few old state statutes restrict this privilege to kill on reasonable appearance of necessity to cases in which the victim stands in a specified close relation to the defender. And some jurisdictions have required the defender in all cases to act at his peril, disallowing the defense if it turns out, contrary to appearances, that the apparent victim was really the aggressor.

Turning now to intentional killings to preserve one's own life or the life of one or more other persons where the person killed is known *not* to be a culpable aggressor, we reach less certain legal ground. First, consider the case where the actor's choice is to take one innocent life in order to save multiple lives. The Model Penal Code found support in the common law for its proposal that one is generally justified in breaking the law where doing so is the only way to avoid an evil the legal system would regard as greater.[8] Although there is authority that denies the extension of this principle to homicidal conduct, the authors of the Model Penal Code meant it to extend here as well, on the footing that the death of two persons is a greater evil than taking the life of one, and there is authority that supports their view.[9]

Where the actor's choice is to take one innocent life in order to save one other, whether himself or someone else, so that reliance upon a numerical calculus of lives is unavailable, the law may not be stated with confidence. Laws and cases on the issues are scarce or nonexistent, and I will have to speak much more speculatively.

I should think we need to distinguish those cases where the person killed constitutes a part (although an innocent part) of the circumstances imperiling the actor, from those where he is a bystander whose life is conscripted in the service of the actor's or another's survival. The first set of cases, the "innocent threat" cases, are those typically in which the threatener is excused or is otherwise nonpunishable and is known to be so by the defender. The threatener may at the time be acting under duress[10] or be legally insane or be a small child. He may even be committing no "legal" action at all, as when one acts in his sleep or when one's body is used as a physical instrument by another. It is fairly clear that one who kills such a person in these circumstances when necessary to save himself is not punishable under Anglo-American law. It is probable, though by no means certain, that his action would be regarded as an instance of justifiable self-defense rather than simply as excusable, and that a third person would be equally justified in intervening on his behalf.[11]

The second set of cases, the "innocent bystander" cases, are those in which one creates a deadly peril to a person uninvolved in one's own peril in order to preserve himself—seizing another to use as a shield against danger, for example. Here there is no authority for finding a justification.

We have so far spoken of actions intended to kill. But actions may take life even if not so intended. How does the criminal law deal with these? The key concepts are recklessness and negligence. Both denote a significant departure from a minimally acceptable standard of care: in the case of recklessness, in awareness of the risk being created; in the case of negligence, in culpable unawareness of it. Whether conduct will be so regarded, and hence be criminal, turns on whether the risk to life it portends is substantial—it need not be highly probable—and whether creating this risk can be justified in terms of the otherwise socially desirable consequences of the conduct and the nonexistence of less risky ways of achieving them.[12] Hence unintentional killing in the course of driving a car is a serious crime if the risk of killing was needlessly increased by highly unsafe driving. But though the mere action of driving a car creates a risk of life, the driver will not be criminally responsible for a resulting death simply on that account. This consequentialist assessment applies even where the risk to life is very great indeed, as in the case of constructing bridges and tunnels, as well as in that of many other routine and accepted activities of modern life. Here, though loss of a certain number of lives could be predicted in advance with very great statistical probability, there is no criminal liability for consequential deaths. Crime is committed only where the persons engaging in the activity can be shown to have created excessive risks that were not inherent in such activity.

Risking just one's own life is another matter. Some statutes prohibit specified activities out of a concern for the risk to those who engage in them. But there is not and never has been any general prohibition against a person risking his life as there once was against his taking it.

The final body of law I shall mention concerns omissions to act, which may, of course, be intentional or unintentional. At the common law one is not criminally obliged to save another's life, no matter how easily he could do so. The principal qualification arises where the law otherwise imposes a duty to act, as in the case of a close relative or where one has agreed to act, explicitly or implicitly.[13] Specific statutes sometimes make punishable the failure to act to rescue a person in peril where one can do so without danger to himself.[14]

ACCOUNTING FOR THE RULES

So much for the map. We are now ready to consider what we can make of it. What underlying principles or patterns of thought can be perceived in this variety of legal rules that prohibit, require, justify, and permit actions that tend to cause death? In the following I will first consider whether and how far the several principles associated with the precept of the sanctity of life can account for the whole of the map of rules. I will then consider particular segments of that map and test the explanatory force of a variety of possible theories.

AN APPROACH THROUGH GENERAL PRINCIPLES:
THE SANCTITY OF LIFE

It is clear, of course, that we value life very highly. Most intentional killings are punishable with the law's most severe sanctions, and even reckless and negligent killings are made criminal. But it is equally clear that we do not give the preservation of life all possible weight. One tradition of thought would give it this weight. I have in mind the sanctity-of-life principle in its strongest sense: the "good and simple moral principle that human life is sacred,"[15] either because it is the gift of God or because of some more general religious commitment, and that it therefore may never be taken by man. One finds these sentiments, for example, in Tolstoy, Schweitzer, and the Buddhist precepts of reverence for life. This absolute view may contribute something to understanding some of our laws, such as the law on suicide and consented killings. But its systematic contradiction by the variety of situations in which the law permits life to be taken and risked suggests that it cannot, at least without qualification, provide an understanding of what is beneath the law.

A variant of this tradition of thought would defend a somewhat weaker version of this principle; namely, that one may never intentionally choose to take the life of another, for whatever end. Thus cases of justified killing have been accounted for on the ground that they do not constitute intentional killings. This argument has its source in the double-effect principle advanced by Saint Thomas Aquinas and other Catholic theologians. It distinguishes two effects of an action, one consisting of what the actor intended, either as an end in itself or as a means to some end, and the other consisting of what he foresaw but did not intend in this sense. In all cases where killing is justified, so the argument runs, there is no intentional choice to take life, because the actor does not, strictly speaking, intend the effect of his action to cause death but is simply aware that his action will have that effect. Thus when one uses deadly force against an assailant to save one's own life, one's action in causing the death of the assailant is not the *intended* effect, but the *known* effect of that action. The intended effect is to remove the threat and no more. The defender, therefore, is not choosing the death of his attacker as a means of preserving his own life but is choosing the only means available to counteract the threat, though aware it will result in the assailant's death.[16]

The doctrine of double effect does not provide that knowing killings may not be serious crimes and wrongs but only that this weaker sense of the sanctity-of-life principle is not necessarily violated when they occur. This weaker version, then, still leaves us uninformed of the *theory* on which killings are justifiable or acceptable when they are not intentional in the strict sense. Beyond that, however, the distinction is so alien to our intuitive common sense as to seem sophistical. For if I shoot a man between the eyes because he is assailing me with upraised dagger, it seems strange to allow me to say I did not choose to take his life, only to prevent the attack. Although the former was not a logically necessary condition of the latter, it was actually necessary in the circumstances, or I, at least, acted on that assumption.[17] Only the ghost of an absolute ban on intended killing is left if it excepts such a killing as this. The double-effect doctrine seems to me much like a fiction in the law, serving to preserve appearances for a principle that has lost its sufficiency.

While one may reject the sanctity-of-life principle in the two senses already discussed, an even weaker sense may still be defended. The principle may be taken to assert not an absolute priority of life or an absolute ban on intentional killing but a presumption in favor of life and against killing so that there can be exceptional circumstances in which the value of life is outweighed by other values or in which killing may be justified on other grounds. This explanation indeed is consistent with the rules of the law, but since it leaves us unenlightened as to what those exceptional circumstances are, it does not greatly advance us.

Another and still weaker sense, however, is not only consistent with the law but undoubtedly demanded by it. Specifically, this sense entails an aspect of the principle of equality: namely, that all human lives must be regarded as having an equal claim to preservation simply because life itself is an irreducible value. Therefore, the value of the particular life, over and above the value of life itself, may not be taken into account. In this sense the sanctity-of-life principle does not purport to say when life may be taken or risked but only requires that in making the judgment certain considerations be ruled out. The life of the good man and the bad stand equal because how a man has led his life may not affect his claim to continued life; the life of the contributing citizen and the dependent or even parasitic one stand equal because knowing how a man will use his remaining life may not affect his claim; and the life of a child and the life of a nonagenarian stand equal because it is irrelevant how much life a person has left.[18] In this sense the principle reflects an important constraint on how we approach judging when life may be taken which we must have in mind as we undertake to disentangle what lies beneath such judgments.

AN APPROACH THROUGH THE PARTICULARS

Let me now change direction in the search for these underlying judgments. Instead of further postulating encompassing principles, I propose to proceed in the tradition of the common-law lawyer, who starts with the cases and sees what he can make of them. In this context that tradition entails considering the particular categories of legal doctrine I put earlier and testing the explanatory force of various possible theories with respect to each.

Intentional Killings of Aggressors.   I consider first the body of laws justifying the intentional killing of one threatening another. When the choice is between the life of the victim and the life of his assailant, the answer is unambiguous in every legal system: the victim may kill to save his life.

It might seem plausible to explain the result in terms of excuse on the view that however much we should prefer people to desist from taking life, even when their own is at risk, the law must take people as they are and no future criminal threat can deter people from acting to meet an immediate threat to their lives. It is very doubtful, however, that this explains Anglo-American law. First, "people as they are" indeed do regard the response as justifiable. Secondly, the explanation is fatally inconsistent with the accepted rule allowing third parties to kill the aggressor, since they are not similarly unamenable to the threat of criminal punishments. One may argue that the excuse rationale is seen partially at work in the rule of some jurisdictions exculpating third-party killings only in cases of actual as opposed to apparent necessity, except when the third person intervenes in behalf of close relatives, where, presumably, deterrence is less workable. But even putting aside that this rule is outmoded and that is was never applicable when the aggressor was committing a felony (which would be true in virtually all cases), what is entailed in this rule is a qualification of the terms on which mistake is available as an excuse (quite possibly out of regard to the enhanced risks of error when a third party intervenes) rather than a judgment that killing the actual aggressor is not justifiable.

Then if such intentional killings are justifiable, on what theory? One possible response is that on the balance of utilities it is better that if one person has to die it should be the attacker rather than his victim. Why is it better? One reason might be that the life of the victim is of greater value than that of the attacker. There are, however, several objections to this explanation. First, it contradicts the equality principle that the lives of all persons must be regarded as of equal value. Second, the rule is not confined to life-against-life situations. As we have seen, defensive killings are justifiable when the interest protected is other than life: prevention of such crimes as kidnapping or rape or even lesser felonies, even when life is not imperiled; or prevention of crimes against property committed after a breaking into one's dwelling or prevention of a deadly assault where the victim can avoid the need to kill by availing himself of a safe retreat. Can the law really be based on a judgment that all such interests are of greater value than a man's life, even a wicked man's? One might reply that the law makes precisely this perverse judgment and that a more enlightened tradition has striven, with some recent success, to confine defensive killings more closely to life-preserving situations. Even conceding this explanation for the moment, one confronts the noncontroverted extension of the rule to cases where several lives are balanced against the life of a single victim. Is it clear that the law's premise is that the lives of two attackers or even twenty are, in total, of less value than the life of the one victim?[19] For surely the rule allows one attacked to kill all his attackers, however numerous they may be. Finally, we run again into the rule that justifies the killing of innocent threats to life as well as culpable ones. On what grounds can the law conceivably be saying that the value of the life of a mentally deranged attacker or of a small child is of less value than the life of the victim?

But one might try to give a more satisfactory answer to why a calculus of social utilities favors defensive killings. One need not say that the life of the victim is a greater good than the lives of his assailants, innocent or not. One can say simply that permitting the victim or a third party to kill in these cases is in the long run "justified as a means to preserving life,"[20] since such action will operate as a sanction against unlawful assaults. Certainly this rationale is plausible, at least if we put aside as perverse legally justified killing in defense of interests other than life.[21] Even so it seems to me to miss the target. First, it proves too much. For if the deterrent threat of deadly preventive force by the victim or an intervenor explains our justifying such killings, it would also support deadly *retaliative* force after the attack was thwarted; yet this extension is plainly not justified under the law. Second, the deterrence rationale proves too little. The argument rests on the contingent fact that justifying deadly defensive force will in the long run save more lives by deterring deadly assaults. But suppose this were not the case. Suppose in some jurisdiction law-enforcement techniques were so perfected that every wrongful attacker would certainly and promptly be convicted and punished with sufficient severity, even perhaps with capital punishment, to exact the maximum deterrent effect possible. In such a jurisdiction preventive killings by the victim or another could not serve the end of preserving life by adding to the deterrent threat against wrongful attacks. Yet is it not inconceivable that deadly defensive force against an attacker would for that reason be denied justification? Surely it would be thought unfair to deny the threatened person the use of justified deadly force against his assailant no matter what was indicated by any long-run, life-preserving calculus, because it is *his* life that is at stake.

This intuitive sense of what fairness requires suggests a quite different approach to understanding what may lie behind the law's justifying intentional killing of aggressors—an approach through the identification of moral rights that require recognition no matter what policy is indicated by a calculus of utilities.

One such approach focuses on the right of the aggressor. Starting with a general right to life possessed by all human beings, the argument is that the aggressor, by his culpable act, forfeits his right to life. This analysis, however, is unsatisfactory on a number of counts. If forfeit means that by his wrongdoing the aggressor allows his life to be taken, it is a Pickwickian sense of "allow" that must be contemplated, since the aggressor would hardly agree that he had any such thing in mind. And even if this difficulty were resolved, there would still be conflict with the accepted principle that one may not, even by an explicit surrender, give up his life or authorize another to take it.[22] On the other hand, forfeit may mean that, wholly apart from what the aggressor may think about the matter, his wrongful act deprives him of any claim he could otherwise make on the basis of his right to life. But to say that his wrongful act deprives him of his right to life is to restate the legal conclusion, and one many question how much it illuminates. First, the theory, in resting forfeiture on wrongdoing, does not explain why the agressor forfeits his right to life during the attack but regains it after the attack has unsuccessfully ended. Second, the theory addresses only the liberty of the victim to kill the aggressor in self-defense; it does not deal with any *right* the victim may have to do so. Suppose, for example, the law did prohibit defensive killings. One's sense of the matter is that such a law would be unjust. Yet the forfeiture theory, as far as it goes, would not impugn such a law or explain why it would be wrong. In other words, the theory tells us why (or rather, that) the aggressor has no moral claim against the deadly force of the victim; it does not tell us why (or even, that) the victim has a right not to be hindered in his use of deadly force against the aggressor. Third, the theory posits that a person does have the general right that others should act in ways that do not imperil his life—a right that the aggressor yields by his action. But such a general right to life is inconsistent with the pattern of the relevant criminal law I have described. Finally, the whole concept of forfeiture by wrongdoing collapses in the case of a threat to life by one who acts without blame—the legally insane attacker or the small child, for example. For, as I pointed out earlier, it probably is the law with us and certainly is the law in many Continental systems that the person attacked may kill such an attacker to the same extent he may kill a culpable aggressor.

As a way of accounting for the law of justified killing of a deadly attacker, a more satisfactory rights approach than the forfeiture concept, which derives only a liberty of the victim to kill from the loss of the aggressor's right to live, is one that derives the liberty from a right against the state. That right, I suggest, is the right of every person to the law's protection against the deadly threats of others. For whatever uncertainty there may be about how much protection must be afforded under this right, it must at least, if it is to have any content, include maintenance of a legal liberty to resist deadly threats by all necessary means, including killing the aggressor. There is, after all, no novelty in positing such a right. The individual does not surrender his fundamental freedom to preserve himself against aggression by the establishment of state authority; this freedom is required by most theories of state legitimacy, whether Hobbesian, Lockeian, or Rawlsian, according to which the individual's surrender of prerogative to the state yields a *quid pro quo* of greater, not lesser, protection against aggression than he had before.[23] This liberty to resist deadly aggression by deadly force and the moral right against the state from which it derives I will refer to as the right to resist aggression.

The recognition of this right accounts for the law of justified killing of aggressors more satisfactorily than other attempts we have considered. The legal right of the victim to kill an aggressor or any number of aggressors when necessary to save his life clearly follows. The explanation requires no concept of forfeiture of the aggressor's rights through his wrongdoing, which, as we saw earlier, was subject to several serious objections. An account of why the aggressor's rights are overridden need not be given because under the theory he has none against his victim. The social and personal value of his life is not diminished by his actions; indeed, when there are multiple aggressors, the good of maximizing lives preserved argues against the victim's defensive actions. But since under this explanation the victim has a right to kill, justice requires that his action be legally justified. Neither has the aggressor any right of his own which is being violated. To say he has a right to life in the circumstances would be incoherent, since it would contradict the theory that gives the victim the right to kill him. What the victim has, as well as any person, is the right to resist aggression against his life, but that right is not violated by the victim who is only defending against the other's aggression.[24] Neither does the theory fail where the person threatening the actor is innocent, as when his action would be excused by the law, because the justification of the victim's defensive action does not arise from the wrongdoing of the threatener but from the right of the victim to preserve his life against a threat to it. The theory is also consistent with the lapse of the right to kill after the threat has ceased, for the right hinges on the presence of the threat. And it is consistent as well with the legal right of a third person to kill the aggressor. In this case, however, the underlying right is not that of the third person, but that of the victim, since the right of the victim to the law's protection would be violated by denying a third person's liberty to intervene as well as by denying the victim's liberty to defend.

But what would this right to resist aggression imply for threats short of the deadly ones I have so far been considering? Is the right limited to deadly threats, or does it include the right to kill to prevent lesser ones?

Two contending principles afford different answers to the question of the extension of the right to resist aggression: the principle of autonomy and the principle of proportionality.[25] According to the first, there should be no limit on the right to resist threats to the person of the actor or interests closely identified therewith. The unrestricted character of the right follows from the corollary of the principle of autonomy of persons that no one may be used as the mere instrument of another, for the essence of physical aggression is that the aggressor seeks so to use the life (taken in this larger sense of person-hood) of the victim. Insofar, then, as the autonomy principle determines the scope of the right to resist aggression, the kinds of interests of personality that may be protected by deadly force are unlimited. It suffices that so much force is necessary to protect the interest. The cost to the aggressor of the victim's exercise of his right so to resist carries no weight. A judgment that the victim could not employ all necessary force to protect personal interests within his autonomy, on the ground that the force needed (killing his aggressor, for example) is excessive, means that the victim's right to defend against aggression is to that extent violated, for he then should be obliged to suffer his being used as a means for the benefit of another against his will.[26]

According to the second principle, the principle of proportionality, the moral right to resist threats is subject to the qualification that the actions necessary to resist the threat must not be out of proportion to the nature of the threat. In compelling this qualification the proportionality principle acknowledges various interests within one's personality and discriminates among them according to degrees of importance. Because the victim has a right to kill his aggressor when necessary to preserve his life, it does not follow that he may do so to protect lesser interests. If killing the aggressor is the only way to save a significantly lesser interest, he must yield it to the aggressor. This qualification is commonly regarded as a principle of justice and is similarly manifested in the range of protective sanctions used by the state to protect various invasions of one's personality. Not all offenses against the person, let alone offenses against his property, carry the severest sanctions. Punishment for offenses generally are scaled in some rough proportion to the enormity of the harm done. It would be thought a basic wrong to the offender, for example, to take his life for a minor theft, and no less a wrong even if it were demonstrable that any lesser punishment would afford less protection against such threats to persons in the community.

I suggest that both of these principles bearing on the extension of the right to resist aggression are reflected in the rules of Anglo-American law. It is the uneasy tension between them that underlies the perennial controversy and changing shape of the law with respect to defining the interests for whose protection one may kill. The proportionality principle is widely in evidence. It is strongly seen in the reform efforts of recent years, such as the proposals of the Model Penal Code, to confine the right to kill generally to cases where killing is necessary to avoid a danger to life.[27] It is also evidenced in more settled provisions of law which, while not so strictly defining proportionality, draw the line at some point on what interests deadly force may be used to protect—for example, the various restraints on killing to protect property, the obligation in many jurisdictions to yield one's ground if by so doing one can avoid the need to kill to save one's life, and even the denial of a right to kill to prevent an unaggravated battery.[28] At the same time, however, the autonomy principle has its influence. Even under recent statutes one may kill to protect one's property where the threat occurs through a forcible entry of one's dwelling. This duty to retreat as a condition of using deadly force has traditionally been a minority rule, and even today many jurisdictions reject it. Indeed, when it is required, there is never a duty to abandon one's home or, in many jurisdictions, similar places like one's place of business. Moreover, despite efforts to confine the use of deadly force to prevent felonies threatening the life of the person, the law of most states continues to permit its use in a much wider range of situations, such as whenever any degree of force is used by the aggressor.

Now it may be argued that these latter rules are reflections not of the autonomy principle but of varying judgments of what interests are proportional to taking the life of the aggressor. The argument has force in cases of killing to prevent crimes like kidnapping and rape, for one may plausibly argue that the interests protected are comparable to that of the victim's life. But one cannot say the same of the interest in remaining where one is, or in protecting one's property from an intruder into one's home, or in preventing any felony whenever some force is used. The strong current of sentiment behind such rules can be understood best as a reflection of the autonomy principle which extends the right to resist aggression broadly to cover threats to the personality of the victim. It is hard to see from where the force behind the elevation of these distinctly lesser interests can come other than from the moral claim of the person to autonomy over his life.

In sum, as far as deadly threats are concerned, the best explanation of the pattern of law governing defensive killing of aggressors is the recognition of the moral right of the victim to kill his aggressor, a right deriving from the right of every person to the fullest protection by the state against such threats. So far as lesser threats are concerned, two contending moral principles are at work: the principle of autonomy, which would extend that moral right to resist aggression to the protection of all facets of the personality of the victim, and the principle of proportionality, which would qualify the extension of that right to interests of the victim commensurate with the life of the aggressor.

Intentional Killing of Bystanders. The remaining category of justified intentional killings I will consider[29] comprises killings committed in the interest of preserving life when the person sacrificed is not a culpable aggressor, or even an innocent one, but a nonthreatening bystander. The one circumstance in which the law arguably justifies killing such a person is that in which killing him is necessary to avoid the certain death of several. This represents the lesser-evil principle we discussed earlier, in which killing one person is deemed a lesser evil than the death of more than one.

It is apparent that the right to resist aggression cannot account for the justification of this type of intentional killing. Neither the actor nor those on whose behalf he acts are threatened in their rights by the one whose life is taken. To use the example of the Model Penal Code itself, the families whose lives are imperiled by the deflection of floodwaters to their homes to avoid the death of a greater number who live in the normal path of the waters are totally uninvolved in the threat to the latter persons. Moreover, the deflection of the waters to their homes is itself an aggressive act against them, which violates their rights not to be used as a means for the benefit of others.[30] When the law justifies this action it therefore violates the right we earlier posited to the state's protection against aggression.[31] That this category of

killings is usually explained in terms of the choice of the lesser
evil suggests its theory of justification: on a judgment of end
results it is better that the fewer number of lives is lost. In the case
of the nonthreatening bystanders, therefore, a balance of utilities
becomes determinative in which the preservation of several lives
justifies the intentional taking of a lesser number even at the cost
of violating a fundamental right the law otherwise recognizes
they possess. That is to say, within this category of killings a force
is at work manifesting a very different notion of right: rightness
in the sense of the desirable social consequence of an action
—whether it will produce a net loss or saving of lives.

But stories tell more than propositions. Suppose a terrorist and
her insane husband and eight-year-old son are operating a ma-
chine-gun emplacement from a flat in an apartment building.
They are about to shoot down a member of the diplomatic corps
whose headquarters the terrorist band is attacking. The victim's
only chance is to throw a hand grenade (which he had earlier
picked up from a fallen terrorist) through his assailants' window.
Probably under Anglo-American law he will be legally justified
in doing so. His right to resist the aggressors' threat is determinative. The value of preserving even the lives of the terrorist, her
legally insane husband, and their infant son carries no weight on
the scale of rights.

Add to the facts that the victim knows there is one person in an
adjoining flat who will surely be killed by the blast. Now he
would *not* be legally justified in throwing the grenade (though he
might be excused), for his action will not result in a net saving of
lives. The right of the person in the adjoining flat who is no part
of the threat against him not to be subjected to his aggression is
therefore determinative.

Finally, assume in addition that the machine gun is being
directed against a companion as well as himself. Under the lesser-
evil doctrine the victim will be legally justified in throwing the
grenade. The right of the person in the adjoining flat is the same,

but that person's claim of right yields to the social valuation that the two other lives are to be preferred over his one life.

This last case reveals the anomaly in the law: that rights prevail over lives in the aggression cases, even multiple or innocent lives, but that lives prevail over rights in the bystander cases like this one, or the flood-deflection case. As suggested above, we must conclude that to the extent this is the law a bystander's right against aggression yields to a utilitarian assessment in terms of net saving of lives. Yet, it should be added, this is not always so, for there are some killings fairly within the net-saving-of-lives, lesser-evil doctrine that it is very doubtful courts would sanction—for example, killing a person to obtain his organs to save the lives of several other people, or even removing them for that purpose against his will without killing him. The unreadiness of the law to justify such aggression against non-threatening bystanders reflects a moral uneasiness with reliance on a utilitarian calculus for assessing the justification of intended killings, even when a net savings of lives is achieved.[32]

Unintentional Killings. I turn now to actions neither intended nor known to cause death which nonetheless create a risk, of which the actor may or may not be aware, that death will result. The law turns the criminality of these actions entirely on a calculus of utilities: how great the probability that life will be lost, how socially important the purposes served by the action, and how feasible the use of less risky measures to achieve the same purpose. While the criminality of intended killings only exceptionally (and, even then, controversially) turns on comparable assessments—that is, in the case of the lesser-evil doctrine—these utilitarian assessments are the standard factors in judging unintended killings. Moreover, this approach to unintended killings is uniformly accepted as sound. It is hard to see how risks to life in the normal processes of living could otherwise be handled by the criminal law, if they are to be handled by it at all.[33] Yet why is it

so obviously commonsensical? Why is there so relatively little tension, so few qualms about actions that create unintended threats to people's lives?

There are differences, surely, between intended and risked killings. Professors Wechsler and Michael, in their classic study of homicide law, pointed them out: "Acts that are intended to kill and capable of causing death are usually highly likely to do so; and they rarely serve ends other than those to which the homicide itself is a means. On the other hand, acts not intended to kill are not, in general, likely to cause death; and even when they are likely to do so, they necessarily serve some other end, which, frequently enough, is desirable."[34] Perhaps this rationale is adequate when risks are moderate; for it is consistent, given a set value on preserving lives, to intervene more protectively against an action, like an intended killing, which carries an extremely high risk, than against actions not so intended which pose a much lesser risk.

Yet I doubt that this rationale is sufficient. As for the first distinction—the likelihood of causing death—so long as an action is intended to kill it counts for nothing that the chance of success in the particular case is not great. The chances of my being struck and killed by a poor marksman with bad eyesight and a crude weapon many yards away are not large. Yet that unlikelihood in no way impairs my right to use deadly force if there is no other way to eliminate that risk. Moreover, some unintended killings create risks as high as most intended ones. When elaborate construction projects are planned—like the Golden Gate Bridge, the Boulder Dam, a tunnel under the English Channel—it can be predicted with a statistical accuracy approaching certainty that a certain number of deaths will result. Nevertheless, we accept the prospect with equanimity and no qualms. We may know that a variety of safety precautions will reduce the number of deaths and, indeed, we often require them—but not always, not when they will cost so much money or time that the effort is deemed disproportionate.[35]

These utilitarian considerations raise the other part of Wechsler and Michael's answer: the social desirability of the bridge or the tunnel or the dam justifies the predicted loss of lives. But this answer generally does not suffice to justify intended killings. Although it is true that intended killings rarely serve ends other than those to which the homicide itself is a means, that is not to say that they may not serve socially desirable ends. When we do justify them on utilitarian grounds—for example, the intentional killing of bystanders—we insist on social goods of an order (usually saving lives) far more compelling than we require to justify risking life, even when the risk is statistically near certain.

Another story will illustrate this last point. An underwater tunnel has been started despite an almost certain loss of five to fifteen lives. Presumably the expected loss is a calculated cost that society is prepared to pay for having the tunnel. At one point a workman is trapped in a section of the partly laid tunnel. A fitting must be lowered into place. If it is laid it will surely crush the workman to death. If it is not laid within an hour—too short a time to effect a rescue—the whole tunnel will have to be abandoned indefinitely, perhaps permanently, because of changing river conditions. I expect that it would nonetheless be a form of criminal homicide to lower the fitting. Even if it were justified under a lesser-evils formula, which is doubtful, the decision would be a soul-searching one. Yet attaining the very same social good—the construction of the tunnel—readily justified its construction despite the predicted loss of multiple lives.

I do not believe, therefore, that the difference in the law of intended and unintended killing can be accounted for in the differences Wechsler and Michael point to. I suggest, rather, that the explanation is to be found in the fundamentally different perspectives we have toward intended and unintended killings. Generally, the former, as I tried to show, are seen as violative of a basic personal right against the state to be protected against the deadly threats of another person. The latter, on the other hand, are not so perceived. Accidental risks to life deriving from the

actions of others tend to be accepted in the same way as risks to life deriving from natural events—as a natural and inevitable contingency of living. We do not have a right against the state to protection against unintended killings, as we do against intended killings. The fundamental urge which animates the claim of right is security against threats directed by others against us, not security against the perils of living. Intentional killings are moral assaults. Risks to life are a part of nature, which under any contractarian view the state has no duty to protect against.

We do not, of course, regard these risks indifferently. They are undesirable and to be avoided, and they are often made criminal, but only when it appears on a utilitarian calculus that the risk is not worth bearing—not at all costs. It is not the degree of risk and the degree of social justification of the respective actions that make the difference. It is that there are not the same moral side constraints on actions that create risk as there are on actions that are seen as aggression. Hence the principle of optimizing end results on a utility calculus has the field entirely.

Yet how can this explanation apply where it is known to a statistical certainty that accidental deaths will result from a course of action, like building a bridge or a tunnel? I have not, after all, argued a distinction between intended and known killings for purposes of defining the extent of the right against acts of aggression. Indeed, I took pains to reject the distinction in discussing the Doctrine of Double Effect. Hence, how can it be that the victims of an unintended killing do not have a right against the state to protection from this present risk of certain death to some of them? One possible answer is that the statistically certain risk created by the construction project is to the workmen who, by agreeing to work on it in return for wages, have consented to the risk. The point has force. Yet it seems insufficient. First, while consent to the risk of death may negate the criminality of a subsequent homicide, it may not do so in cases of intentional killings. Why, then, given our rejection of the distinction between intended and known killings, should consent negate

the criminality of homicide in the cases of known killings in these examples? Some further explanation is needed. Second, the absence of consent does not appear determinative in these cases. The statistically certain risk of death produced by the widespread use of the automobile and attendant services, for example, is not confined to those who choose to drive.

The further necessary explanation, I suggest, lies in the nature of statistical knowledge. It is known that some people will be killed; it is not known who they will be. If statistical analysis determines that ten out of a thousand will die, no individual person can claim that his death is a known consequence of the action. His own risk, indeed, is relatively modest—in this case one percent. So it is that in these cases the known deaths need only be regarded as a regrettable cost and not as the perpetration of an injustice.

Omissions. I turn finally to the omission cases, the last piece in the puzzle. Though failing to act while knowing that a death will thereby result might be justified or not in the same way as affirmative actions, the law treats omissions differently. Affirmative actions which cause or tend to cause the death of a person are culpable or not depending on an inquiry into their justification (putting aside excuse). With omissions to act no such inquiry arises until a duty to act is first established. Hence a person is at liberty knowingly to permit another to die, without regard to any consideration of whether his omission is justified, unless the law otherwise imposes a duty to act, as it may, for example, because of a status, contractual, or equitable relationship between the parties. On what theory can the law be explained?

One view is that the criminal law is unable to formulate a rule commanding when a person must act without being so indefinite as to render its administration uncertain and unjust. For how could one formulate a rule that would say just how far a person need alter his life or burden himself and those dependent upon him in order to save the life of a person in need? And how could the rule distinguish those who must do so out of the many who could, at varying costs, do so as well? This emphasis on indefiniteness is the classic justification for requiring action only when the law otherwise imposes a duty to act.[36]

Certainly this explanation has some merit. In addition to its intrinsic plausibility it tends to be borne out by occasional general statutes that require the nondangerous rescue of a person in distress and those that require action in a variety of particular situations (like registering for the draft and filing income-tax returns), for in these instances a sufficiently definite rule is practicable. Yet one may doubt that it represents the whole story. To be sure, any general formulation of a requirement to act—for example, one based on an appeal to common decency—would be indefinite; but, as has been persuasively argued,[37] it would be no more indefinite than the standard of criminal liability for reckless or negligent killings, which also turns on an assessment of such imponderables as necessity of means, desirability of ends, and probability of death.[38]

An additional possible explanation is the undesirability of people sacrificing their own interests, no matter how slight, to aid another person, even where that person otherwise will die. We need not pause over this view. It obviously contradicts the elemental humanitarianism that permeates our culture. A lesser version of this view is that while it is desirable for people to act to keep another alive, it is not desirable for the criminal law to seek to make them do so. But one wonders why not. One possible reason is that a general affirmative duty to act would necessitate unacceptably indefinite standards of conduct. I have already said why I think this would not be so. Another possible reason is that such an affirmative duty could not affect people's conduct. But surely deterring inaction is not intrinsically more difficult than deterring acts, even acknowledging the greater difficulty of proving the *mens rea*—the state of mind— that accompanies an omission.[39] Another reason might be the general undesirability of using the criminal law to coerce virtuousness.[40] But compelling actions to save life is hardly using punishment to exact private conformity to virtue or to standards of good conduct that are at all controversial.

What, then, is the further explanation of the law's traditional reluctance to criminalize omissions? I believe an approach through a rights analysis casts light on the question. On the one hand, the moral right to resist aggression hardly provides the basis for a claim on others to their help;[41] the failure to assist another in need is not the type of aggressive threat to personality that gives rise to a claim against the state for protection. Hence, one finds the pervasive distinction, in the law as elsewhere, between killing a person, which does violate his right, and letting him die, which does not.[42] On the other hand, the right to resist aggression rests to some extent, as we saw above when dealing with deadly defensive force against nondeadly threats, upon the notion of autonomy, which posits a person's right not to be used coercively in the service of another. Requiring actions of bystanders to save others tends to collide with the autonomy principle. For to accord to a stranger a claim upon me that does not flow in any sense from my own actions conscripts the uses of my life to his.[43] This explanation, it may be observed, is consistent with the exceptional cases in which the common law does traditionally compel action—cases of status, contractual, or equitable relationship between the parties. In these cases the putative helper, by his actions, has implicated himself in the predicament of the person in need, and he cannot make the same claim of autonomy.[44]

Of course, this autonomy principle does not have the field to itself. We saw earlier how the principle of proportionality contends with it in cases of resistance to nondeadly threats to the person. The proportionality principle does so also in cases of omissions where, in a variety of situations, usually statutory (for example, the statutes requiring the giving of aid to one in distress where there is practically no risk to the aider), the demands of the principle of autonomy are compromised on a judgment of gross disproportion between what is demanded of the aider and what is at stake for the person in need.

SUMMARY

So much, then, is the map of the criminal law and what I suggest to be some of the moral sentiments and the perceptions of actions and events that explain its contours. The sacredness of human life is an important ingredient of the humanistic ideal. Insofar as it asserts the equality-of-lives principle it constitutes a significant influence on the law. In any other sense it does not. We have to look elsewhere to comprehend the determinative influences on the shape of the law.

One predominant and persistent theme is the conception of the rightness of actions—rightness measured not by what most effectively preserves lives or by what best serves the social interest of all, but by what a person may claim as his due equally with all other persons. The right, in this sense, to resist aggression, embracing the liberty to use defensive force and the right to the law's protection against aggression, from which the liberty derives, plays a central role in explaining the shape of the law. When the victim must take the life of one threatening his own in order to survive, his action is justifiable, whether the persons he must kill are one or many, guilty or innocent, so long as they are part of the threat. But other principles of right manifest themselves in other situations where life is at stake. Where interests other than the victim's life (or interests closely identified with it) are threatened, two competing principles affect his right to kill: the principle of autonomy, which would extend the right to resist aggression to all threats to the personality of the victim, and the principle of proportionality, which would draw the line at preservation of life and closely identified interests. Neither principle governs entirely in the law. Further, in cases of omissions to act to avoid the death of another, there is a similar tension between these principles operating in the law.

But explanations in terms of rights and principles fail to account for the whole shape of the law. Another force is at work manifesting a very different notion of right: rightness in the sense of the desirable consequence of an action—whether it will produce a net loss or saving of lives, whether it will serve or disserve prevailing estimates of social goods other than saving lives. This competing standard, turning solely on evaluation of consequences, is manifested in the lesser-evil doctrine. When taking the life of an innocent nonthreatening bystander will result in a net saving of lives, the law justifies an actor in doing so, notwithstanding the invasion of the bystander's own right to the law's protection against aggression. As we saw, the doctrine, when carried to its logical conclusion, is controversial, further reflecting the tensions in the impulses that shape our law.

This consequentialist standard is most firmly in evidence when unintended killing is involved, for here no individual rights are perceived which must be subordinated or qualified. It is in these cases that the value we place on life as against other goods and interests may be most clearly seen, since no competing principle of right exists to complicate its assessment. It is revealing that the judgments in this area that appeal most immediately to our common sense permit life to be yielded when the costs of saving it, in terms of the comforts, conveniences, and satisfactions of many, seem too high.[45] The nature of the action that takes life commands our concern far more than loss of life itself.[46]

These, then, appear to be the underlying principles and controlling patterns of thought that govern the law's judgments of life-taking actions. The principles and patterns I have identified do not all fit into a harmonious pattern; inconsistencies and tensions, reflecting a variety of impulses and perceptions, appear to me a major feature of our experience. Whether, to that extent, what I have concluded is defective as a theory of the criminal law depends on what constitute the governing criteria of a proper theory of this kind. While I could not properly address that issue here, I would venture two brief comments. First, I recognize that it may well be possible to discern a rationale underlying our criminal-law tradition that achieves a more logically consistent explanation of the whole than what I have produced. I offer only my best effort. Secondly, I am dubious that any single, self-consistent theory is likely ever to comprehend the whole of our experience. I venture the intuition that the essential stuff of our moral judgments and perceptions in complex matters like the taking of life is tension and contradiction that may be identified but never dissolved.

CONCLUDING OBSERVATIONS

I should like to conclude by saying a few words on how this pattern of principles and perceptions bears on some of the controversial issues of the day I mentioned at the outset. Since my focus throughout has been on the law, I will confine myself to those issues that pose a problem for the criminal law and ask no more than how the principles and perceptions which, I have argued, underlie the shape of our criminal law bear on those issues.

Human medical experimentation seems to me, as it has to others,[47] not readily distinguishable from other cases where life may be legally risked to achieve some greater social good. Indeed, if a bridge justifies the predicted loss of life its construction entails, surely the saving of countless lives through medical discoveries does so as well. Since loss of life is risked, not intended, no right is invaded in either case. And since the subject consents to a risk of death rather than to being killed, there is no ground for denying the efficacy of the consent. The key problem for the law is not intrinsic but administrative—how to assure that risks are minimized, that consent is freely given, that the competence of the experimenter and the promise of the experiment justify the risk, and that abuses are avoided.

The criminalization of abortion is a different matter. Whether a fetus must be regarded as a person and at what stage is a threshold question little illumined by the themes we have found dominant in shaping the law. But once that threshold is passed and personhood recognized in a fetus at some stage, the abortion debate turns quite centrally on a number of those themes. How cogently may the dependent fetus be analogized to a person requiring affirmative aid from another to survive, aid to which it has no claim of right? Even if so analogized, has the mother's participation invested her with a duty not to let it die? How far may the answer turn on whether she at first sought the child, whether she was just careless, or whether she had been raped? Is the whole analogy to letting die by failing to aid misconceived because abortion entails affirmative action to stop life-sustaining aid already flowing? In other words, is it more like turning off a machine that is keeping a person alive than failing to attach the person to it in the first place? Even if so, how much does it weigh that it is *her* person—her "machine"—over which she has autonomy? Where the pregnancy is endangering her very existence, may the fetus be regarded as an innocent threat against which she may defend herself with whatever means are necessary? Where the fetus poses a threat "only" to her psychological well-being, does the principle of proportionality argue against taking the fetus's life, or should her interests of personality be defined broadly so that the principle of autonomy would control? Finally, whatever the claims of justice in recognizing rights, how far do consequentialist considerations of achieving some optimal set of socially desirable results require their subordination? I am not so foolhardy as to venture answers at this point. My purpose is only to point out what is apparent in much of the abortion literature[48]—that the underlying themes we found at work in doctrines of the criminal law bear centrally on the current controversy over the criminalization of abortion.

The human transplant problem also raises several of these themes. In a suitable case, may the organs of a unique donor be removed against his will to save the lives of several? Probably, as I suggested earlier, the rights principle would be strong enough to resist legalizing such an action, but the lesser-evil principle, in its broadest reach, would point the other way. Where the donor consents at some risk to his life, the legal problems again, as in the case of medical experimentation, would be administrative. Where removing his organ would kill him one faces the engrained reluctance to sanction taking one's own life or permitting another to do so. Where the donor is moribund two main problems emerge. The first is whether one with virtually no life left may be treated as dead, as no longer a person, for purposes of the criminal law. An affirmative answer would entail a serious breach of the equality-of-lives principle. The second problem is determining when a person is dead, just as the abortion issue raises the problem of when a person begins to live. Here again legal experience offers little guidance since the beginning and ending of life were generally regarded in the law as unproblematic events. Only recent scientific sophistication has fully revealed the gradualness of the process both of man's coming into being and his ceasing to be, and therefore has exposed the troubling choices that the law cannot eventually escape making.[49]

Euthanasia also involves the equality-of-life principle: May life be treated differently when it becomes unwanted and unbearable by the person, or must life, as life, always be treated equally, so that a judgment of its worth, even by the person himself, may never enter into a justification for taking it? May the lesser-evil rationale justify some qualification of the equality-of-life principle when death is certain and imminent in any event, and killing would save the person from the evil of a few moments of agonizing pain and terror?[50]

A FINAL COMMENT

Using the rules of the criminal law as a guide, I have tried in this essay to identify some of the underlying principles and controlling patterns of thought that govern our judgments of life-taking actions and to suggest their relevance to a number of controversial problems involving the taking of life. I took my task to be descriptive and analytical, not judgmental; to state, that is, what the controlling principles and patterns are in fact, not whether they are sound (whatever sound might mean) or whether some are sounder than others. But of course these judgmental issues are the ultimate ones. Should the sanctity-of-life ideal prevail over rights and a calculus of other utilities, or does it represent a religious commitment that may not be given primacy in a secular, or at least a pluralistic, society? Should rights always prevail because they express a commitment to justice, or is the notion of justice they express a product of man's primordial fears, conditioning, and genetic structuring over time which a rational order should seek to overcome?[1] Is a consequentialist principle to be preferred because it nondogmatically opens the assessment to embrace the widest range of social utilities at any time and place, or is the final commitment to socially desirable consequences itself a dogma that should be rejected insofar as it denies the primacy of life and the claims of justice? I have not ventured to say, mainly because I do not know. These questions are, after all, at the core of the great controversies in moral philosophy. I have to be content with having shown how it is that even a criminal lawyer reaches them at the end.

NOTES

1. H. L. A. Hart, *The Concept of Law* (Oxford: Oxford University Press 1961), p. 188.

2. Ibid., p. 189.

3. See Austin, "A Plea for Excuses," *Proceedings of the Aristotelian Society* 57 (1956–57): 1–2. As an example, compare section 53.1 of the recently superseded German Penal Code of 1871, which provided that, "No act constitutes an offense if it was necessary in self-defense or in defense of another," with section 53.3, which provided that, "Excessive self-defense or defense of another is not punishable if the perpetrator has exceeded the limits of defense by reason of consternation, fear or fright." *The American Series of Foreign Penal Codes, The German Penal Code of 1871* 4 (1961): 41–42.

4. I have chosen not to burden these notes with complete citations to authority for the well-known legal doctrines discussed. See generally W. LaFave and A. Scott, *Criminal Law* (Minneapolis: West Publishing Co., 1972), 381–407. *Model Penal Code* §*3.01–.12, Comments* (Tent. Draft No. 8, 1958); Note, *"Justification for the Use of Force in the Criminal Law,"* Stan. L. Rev. 13 (1961): 566; Note, "Justification: The Impact of the Model Penal Code on Statutory Reform," *Colum. L.Rev.* 75 (1975): 914.

5. See the opinion of Justices Brennan and Marshall in Furman v. Georgia, 408 U.S. 238 (1972).

6. It is noteworthy that popular sentiment in some states compelled reinstatement of capital punishment after courts invalidated it for a variety of reasons. In California voters reinstated the death penalty by a two-to-one vote in a popular referendum held after the California Supreme Court held it unconstitutional. See "Note on the Constitutional Status of Capital Punishment," in S. Kadish and M. Paulsen, *Criminal Law and its Processes,* 3d ed. (Boston: Little, Brown, 1975), p. 209. It is also noteworthy that capital punishment is sanctioned in the European Convention on Human Rights. Article 2(1) provides: "Everyone's right to life shall be protected by law. No one shall be deprived of his life intentionally save in the execution of a sentence of a court following his conviction of a crime for which this penalty is provided by law," *Council of Europe, Eur. Conv. on Human Rights, Collected Texts,* 8th ed. (1972).

7. See *Model Penal Code* §§3.07(2)(b),(3) (Proposed Official Draft 1962); Note, "Justification: The impact of the Model Penal Code on Statutory Reform," n. 4 above. The older tradition of the common law, found also in some European countries, allowing a broader privilege to kill for law-enforcement purposes, is reflected in the European Convention on Human Rights, Art. 2(2): "Deprivation of life shall not be regarded as inflicted in contravention of this Article [see n. 6 above] when it results from the use of force which is no more than absolutely necessary: (a) in defense of any person from unlawful violence; (b) in order to effect a lawful arrest or prevent the escape of a person lawfully detained; (c) in action lawfully taken for the purpose of quelling a riot or insurrection." *Council of Europe,* n. 6 above.

8. *Model Penal Code* §3.02, Comment at 6 (Tent. Draft No. 8, 1958).

9. The commentary to section 3.02 of the Model Penal Code states: "[R]ecognizing that the sanctity of life has a supreme place in the hierarchy of values, it is nonetheless true that conduct which results in taking life may promote the very value sought to be protected by the law of homicide. Suppose, for example, that the actor has made a breach in the dike, knowing that this will inundate a farm, but taking the only course available to save a whole town. If he is charged with homicide of the inhabitants of the farm house, he can rightly point out that the object of the law of homicide is to save life, and that by his conduct he has effected a net saving of innocent lives. The life of every individual must be assumed in such a case to be of equal value and the numerical preponderance in the lives saved compared to those sacrificed surely establishes an ethical and legal justification for the act. . . . So too a mountaineer, roped to a companion who has fallen over a precipice, who holds on as long as possible but eventually cuts the rope, must certainly be granted the defense that he accelerated one death slightly but avoided the only alternative, the certain death of both." *Model Penal Code* §3.02, Comment at 8 (Tent. Draft No. 8, 1958).

A number of states have recently adopted formulations of the lesser-evil principle as parts of their criminal codes. See Note, "Justification: The Impact of the Model Penal Code on Statutory Reform," n. 4 above. Wisconsin, however excludes homicidal actions. See *Wis. Stat. Ann.* §939 47 (1958). And compare Fletcher, "The Individualization of Excusing Conditions," *S. Cal. L. Rev.* 47 (1974): 1269, 1278: "German scholars, influenced by the Kantian tradition, have rejected the possibility of justification where the act is one of killing an innocent person."

10. Insofar as duress may excuse homicidal conduct. It often may not, e.g., *Cal. Penal Code* §26 (Minneapolis: West Publishing Co., 1970). See also W. LaFave and A. Scott, *Criminal Law* (1972), p. 376.

11. As Professor Fletcher has observed, the issue has not squarely been faced in the Anglo-American law. G. Fletcher, "Proportionality and the Psychotic Aggressor: A Vignette in Comparative Criminal Theory," *Israel L. Rev.* 8 (1973): 367, 370. The Model Penal Code does allow the use of necessary defensive force in these cases. See its definition of "unlawful force" against which defensive measures are privileged. Model Penal Code §3.11(1) (Proposed Official Draft 1962).

The commentary to this section states: "The reason for legitimizing protective force extends to cases where the force it is employed against is neither criminal nor actionable—so long as it is not affirmatively privileged. It must, for example, be permissible to defend against attacks by lunatics or children and defenses to liability such as duress, family relationship or diplomatic status are plainly immaterial. We think that it is also immaterial that other elements of culpability, e.g., intent or negligence, are absent. Whatever may be thought in tort, it cannot be regarded as a crime to safeguard an innocent person, whether the actor or another, against threatened death or injury which is unprivileged, even though the source of the threat is free from fault." Ibid., §3.04, Comment 5, at 29 (Tent. Draft No. 8, 1958).

Also supporting the right to take all necessary defensive measures, see G. Radbruch, "Jurisprudence in the Criminal Law," *J. Comp. Leg. & Int'l L.* 18 (3d ser., 1936): 212, 218; J. Smith & B. Hogan, *Criminal Law*, 3d ed. (1973) p. 262. Professor Noonan has suggested that Aquinas found justifiable the killing of an innocent person in self-defense. Noonan, "An Almost Absolute Value in History," in *The Morality of Abortion*, ed. Noonan (Cambridge, Mass.: Harvard University Press, 1970), pp. 24–25.

12. See Wechsler and Michael, "A Rationale of the Law of Homicide: I," *Colum. L. Rev.* 37 (1937): 701, 744, identifying the relevant factors as, "(1) the probability that death or serious injury will result; (2) the probability that the act will also have desirable results and the degree of their desirability, in the determination of which the actor's purposes are relevant; (3) if the act serves desirable ends, its efficacy as a means, as opposed to the efficacy of other and less dangerous means."

13. See G. Hughes, "Criminal Omissions," *Yale L. J.* 67 (1958): 590.

14. See F. J. M. Feldbrugge, "Good and Bad Samaritans: A Comparative Survey of Criminal Law Provisions Concerning Failure to Rescue," *Am. J. Comp. L.* 14 (1966): 630.

15. Working Party, Board for Social Responsibility, Church of England, *On Dying Well: An Anglican Contribution to the Debate on Euthanasia*, (Church Information Office, 1975), p. 24.

16. See John Finnis, "The Rights and Wrongs of Abortion: A Reply to Judith Thompson," *Phil. & Pub. Affairs* 2# (1973): 117, 138-39. Philippa Foot, "The Problem of Abortion and the Doctrine of Double Effect," *Oxford Rev.* 5 (1967): 5, See also G. Grisez, *Abortion: The Myths, the Realities and the Arguments* (New York: Corpus Books, 1970), pp. 267-346.

17. See Professor H. L. A. Hart's trenchant critique of the Doctrine of Double Effect in his *Punishment and Responsibility* (1968), pp. 124-125.

18. The once-popular philosopher, Joseph Popper-Lynkeus developed this theme. See the entry on him by Paul Edwards in *The Encyclopedia of Philosophy* vol. 6, ed. P. Edwards (1967), pp. 401, 403.

Edwards paraphrases a passage of Popper's as follows: "Let us suppose that the angel of death were to allow Shakespeare and Newton, in the most creative periods of their lives, to go on living only on condition that we surrender to him 'two stupid day-laborers or even two incorrigible thieves.' As moral beings we must not so much as consider an exchange of this kind. It would be far better if Shakespeare and Newton were to die. One may call attention, as much as one wishes, to the pleasure produced in countless future ages by Shakespeare's plays; one may point to the immense progress of science which would be the consequence of the prolongation of Newton's life—by comparison with the sacrifice of a human being, these are mere 'luxury values.' "

19. Compare the following observations of Paul Edwards on Popper-Lynkeus's views: "In one place Popper goes so far as to assert that it would be better if all the aggressors in the world, even if they numbered millions, were to be destroyed than if a single human being succumbed to them without resistance." Ibid., p. 403.

20. Wechsler and Michael, n. 12 above, p. 739.

21. As Wechsler and Michael point out: "The most obvious case of homicidal behavior that serves the end of preserving life is that of the victim of a wrongful attack who finds it necessary to kill his assailant to save his own life. We need not pause to reconsider the universal judgment that there is no social interest in preserving the lives of aggressors at the cost of those of their victims. Given the choice that must be made, the only defensible policy is one that will operate as a sanction against unlawful aggression." Ibid., p. 736.

22. One finds, for example, in Locke and Blackstone the two conflicting assertions that one may not alienate his right to life (J. Locke, "The Second Treatise of Government," *Two Treatises of Government* §6, p. 288-89, §135, p. 375-76 [P. Laslett ed. 1960]; W. Blackstone, *Commentaries*, Vol. 4, p. 189), but that one may forfeit that right by his actions (J. Locke, ibid., §23, p. 302, §172, pp. 400-401; W. Blackstone, ibid., Vol. 1, p. 133). See the discussion in Bedau, "The Right to Life," *Monist* 52 (1968): 550, 567.

23. Professor R. Nozick finds the basis of all moral side constraints on actions, as well as of the particular side constraint that prohibits aggression against another, in "the fact of our separate existences" and the "root idea . . . that there are different individuals with separate lives and so no one may be sacrificed for others." R. Nozick, *Anarchy, State and Utopia* (New York; Basic Books, 1974), p. 33.

24. Cf. ibid., p. 34; I. Kant, *The Metaphysical Elements of Justice*, trans. J. Ladd (1965), pp. 35-36.

25. For an illuminating treatment of these contending principles see Fletcher, "Proportionality and the Psychotic Aggressor: A Vignette in Comparative Criminal Theory," *Israel L. Rev.* 8 (1973): 367, 376–90.

26. So much appears to be reflected by the law of Germany and the Soviet Union which, in resisting formal recognition of any such general limitation on the use of necessary deadly force, manifest the force of the autonomy principle. Ibid., pp. 368, 381.

27. *Model Penal Code*, Proposed Official Draft, §§3.04(2)(b), 3.06(3)(d), 307(2)(b).

28. See, e.g., People v. Jones, 191 Cal. App. 2 d 478, 12 Cal. Rptr. 777 (2d Dist., 1961), in which the court held it no defense to a wife charged with manslaughter of her husband that killing him was her only means to stop his slapping assault on her.

29. I am putting aside capital punishment and the killing of fleeing felons. Both involve either a weighing of utilities—the good of law enforcement versus the good of preserving lives—or the issue of the retributive right of the state to punish. A discussion of these issues would largely illustrate further the dominant themes already indicated in the areas of law covered in this paper.

30. See, generally, Murphy, "The Killing of the Innocent," *Monist* 54 (1973): 527.

31. It is true that the nonthreatening bystander—like the families toward whose homes the floods are deflected—may possibly have a legal right to resist persons attempting the deflection. It is somewhat strange, but not illogical, to extend a right to the victim to resist, while at the same time freeing the attacker from criminal liability. Even if the law extends this right to the victim, however, the law is still *partly* violating his right against aggression, which includes the right against the state that the aggressive conduct be criminally prohibited.

32. It is worth observing that some instances of the net-saving-of-lives principle do not produce this conflict. One such instance was suggested by Mrs. Foot, n. 16 above, p. 9: A physician denies his limited quantity of medicine to one person who needs all of it to survive in order to use it for five persons each of whom requires one-fifth the supply to be saved. For reasons we shall see when we reach omissions (involving the distinction between letting someone die and killing him), none of the ill persons has a right over any of the others to receive the medicine. A similar instance is presented by the often discussed hostage cases in which a band threatens to kill two persons in their power in order to obtain the death of one person in the custody of another group. Consistent with a rights approach, the group may desist from protecting the wanted person and permit the band to enter and kill him, for in doing so they will effect a net saving of lives and violate no one's rights. Contrariwise, it would be inconsistent with the rights approach were they themselves to kill the one person in their custody.

An instance of a quite different kind is suggested in the Commentary to the Model Penal Code itself: "[A] mountaineer, roped to a companion who has fallen over a precipice, who holds on as long as possible but eventually cuts the rope, must certainly be granted the defense" of the net-savings-of-lives principle "because the only alternative was the certain death of both." *Model Penal Code* §3.02, Comment at 8 (Tent. Draft No. 8, 1958). Here, however, the dangling mountaineer is no bystander. He constitutes a threat, although an innocent one, so that the right to resist aggression suffices to justify cutting the rope.

33. There is disagreement over the justification for imposing criminal liability on the basis of negligence. *Compare* Hall, "Negligent Behavior Should Be Excluded from Penal Liability," *Colum. L. Rev.* 63 (1963): 632, with H. L. A. Hart, n. 17 above, p. 152 (1968).

34. Wechsler and Michael, n. 12 above, p. 742.

35. For an insightful examination of this aspect of the prevailing response to life-threatening conduct see Calabresi, "Reflections on Medical Experimentation in Humans," *Daedalus* 98 (1969): 387.

36. See Macaulay, *A Penal Code Prepared by the Indian Law Commissioners,* Note M, 53–56 (1837).

37. Wechsler and Michael, n. 12 above, p. 751, n. 175.

38. See ibid., p. 751, n. 175: "Whereas the issue [in liability for negligent acts] is . . . whether or not the act is a sufficiently necessary means to sufficiently desirable ends to compensate for the risk of death or injury which it creates, the issue [in liability for omissions] is whether or not freedom to remain inactive serves ends that are sufficiently desirable to compensate for the evil that inaction permits to befall. The extent of the burden imposed by the act is obviously a relevant factor in making such an evaluation. If the burden is negligible or very light, the case for liability is strong, and the difficulty of formulating a general rule no more insuperable an obstacle than in the case of acts."

39. See ibid., p. 751, n. 175.

40. See Skolnick, "Coercion to Virtue," *S. Cal. L. Rev.* 41 (1968): 588.

41. See Murphy, "The Killing of the Innocent," *Monist* 54 (1973): 527, 546. "When a man has a right, he has a claim against interference. Simply to refuse to be beneficent to him is not an invasion of his rights because it is not to interfere with him at all."

42. See Foot, note 16 above, p. 11: "Most of us allow people to die of starvation in India and Africa, and there is surely something wrong with us that we do; it would be nonsense, however, to pretend that it is only in law that we make a distinction between allowing people in the underdeveloped countries to die of starvation and sending them poisoned food. Th:re is worked into our moral system a distinction between what we owe people in the form of aid and what we owe them in the way of non-interference."

It is worth noting in passing that this theory is not applicable to governments, which, unlike the people subject to them, are precisely instruments to be used by such people. For example, the Universal Declaration of Human Rights, in Articles 22, 24, 25, and 26, asserts a person's rights against his government to be provided with a variety of social services. G. A. Res. 217, U.N. Doc. A/810 at 71, 75, 76 (1948). The theory is quite applicable, however, to the relation between governments and persons belonging to other governments. On this view the issue of the wealthier countries of the world feeding the starving ones is an issue of beneficence, not rights.

43. In suggesting that one may have a right to decline to do an act that we should criticize him for not doing, there is no inconsistency. As Professor R. Dworkin suggests, when we say a person has a right to do something (or not to do

it), we imply that it would be wrong to require him to do it. But it is consistent to say that that which he has a right to do (or not to do) in this sense is still not the right thing for him to do. Dworkin, "Taking Rights Seriously," in E. Rostow, ed., *Is Law Dead?* (1975), pp. 168, 174.

44. See S. Kadish and M. Paulsen, *Criminal Law and its Processes,* 3d ed. (1975), p. 85.

45. Compare J. Hospers, *Human Conduct* (1963), pp. 399–400: "Some philosophers, such as Kant, have said that an individual human life is a thing not only of great value but of *infinite* value—that to preserve one human life it would be worthwhile not indeed to risk the collapse of civilization (for that would involve the loss of many lives), but to sacrifice for all mankind some convenience or source of happiness that would *not* involve the loss of life."

46. See Calabresi, n. 35 above, p. 388: "Accident law indicates that our commitment to human life is not, in fact, so great as we say it is; that our commitment to life-destroying material progress and comfort is greater. But this fact merely accentuates our need to make a bow in the direction of our commitment to the sanctity of human life (whenever we can do so at a reasonable total cost). It also accentuates our need to reject any societal decisions that too blatantly contradict this commitment. Like 'free will,' it may be less important that this commitment be total than that we believe it to be there."

47. See Calabresi, n. 35 above, p. 391.

48. E.g., Thomson, "A Defense of Abortion," *Phil. & Pub. Affairs* 1 (1971): 47. Finnis, "The Rights and Wrongs of Abortion," n. 16 above; Foot, "The Problem of Abortion and the Doctrine of Double Effect," n. 16 above; Brody, "Abortion and the Sanctity of Life," *Amer. Phil. Q.* 10 (1973): 133.

49. In saying that the problem is revealed by scientific discoveries, I do not want it taken as agreeing with those who seem to suggest that the problem is answerable by such discoveries. See, e.g., P. Stein & J. Shand, *Legal Values in Western Society,* 171, n. 36 (1974). Roe v. Wade, 410 U.S. 113, 220 (1973) (Douglas, J., concurring). Who is to be regarded as no longer a person for purposes of legal and moral judgment is hardly a scientific question. See generally Wertheimer, "Understanding the Abortion Argument," *Phil. & Pub. Affairs* I (1971): 67.

50. See *On Dying Well,* n. 15 above, p. 58, where the example is given of shooting a man trapped in a burning gun turret. The Report comments: "Life is thereby shortened by only a matter of moments, and great agony of short duration is avoided or terminated. Can it be successfully argued that the evil asserted (great agony) is greater than the evil inflicted (death)?"

51. See, generally, Scarf, "The Anatomy of Fear," *N.Y. Times Magazine,* 16 June 1974, p. 10.

ABOUT THE CONTRIBUTORS

Owsei Temkin is William H. Welch professor emeritus of the history of medicine at The Johns Hopkins University. He holds the M.D. degree and is well known for his scholarly publications in medical history. These include *The Falling Sickness* (2d ed., 1971), *Soranus' Gynecology* (1956), *Galenism* (1973), and *The Double Face of Janus and Other Essays in the History of Medicine* (1977).

William K. Frankena is professor of philosophy at the University of Michigan. He has been president of the American Philosophical Association (Western Division), and was chosen by it to serve as Carus Lecturer (1972-73). He has written numerous articles in moral philosophy, and his books include *Ethics* (1963), *Three Historical Philosophies of Education* (1965), *Some Beliefs about Justice* (1966), and *Moral Scepticism and Moral Principles* (1973).

Sanford H. Kadish is Dean and Alexander and May T. Morrison Professor of Law at the School of Law of the University of California, Berkeley. His active career has included service as president of the American Association of University Professors (1970-72). He has written numerous articles on legal issues and, in addition, is coauthor of *Criminal Law and Its Processes* (3d ed., 1975), *Dimensions of Academic Freedom* (1969), and *Discretion to Disobey: A Study of Lawful Departures from Legal Rules* (1973).

INDEX

The Johns Hopkins University Press

*This book was composed in Baskerville text and
display type by Jones Composition Company Inc.,
from a design by Patrick Turner. It was printed
on 55 lb. Antique Cream paper and bound in
Joanna Arrestox cloth by the Maple Press Company.*